The Candle Factory

This book is dedicated to Tom Hyland, from Ballyfermot in Dublin, who helped found the East Timor Ireland Solidarity Campaign. His tireless work, and the effort and commitment of all those associated with the campaign, has in no small way helped to keep the terrible plight of that downtrodden country at centre stage in the international arena.

The Candle Factory

Five Hundred Years
of Rathborne's, Master Chandlers

BERNARD NEARY

THE LILLIPUT PRESS
in association with
JOHN G. RATHBORNE LTD

All maps courtesy of and copyright
Phoenix Maps, 26 Ashington Avenue,
Navan Road, Dublin 7

First published 1998 by
THE LILLIPUT PRESS LTD
62-63 Sitric Road, Arbour Hill
Dublin 7, Ireland
E-MAIL: lilliput@indigo.ie
Web site: http://indigo.ie/~lilliput

in association with

JOHN G. RATHBORNE LTD

A CIP record for this title is available from
The British Library.

ISBN 1-901866-27-0

Set in 11.5 on 15 Janson
Display heads in 24 Janson Italic

Typeset by
Typeform Repro Limited
East Wall Road, Dublin 3
Phone 855 3855

Printed in Ireland by
Future Print Limited
103 Grangeway, Baldoyle Industrial Estate, Dublin
Telephone 01-839 2070

Contents

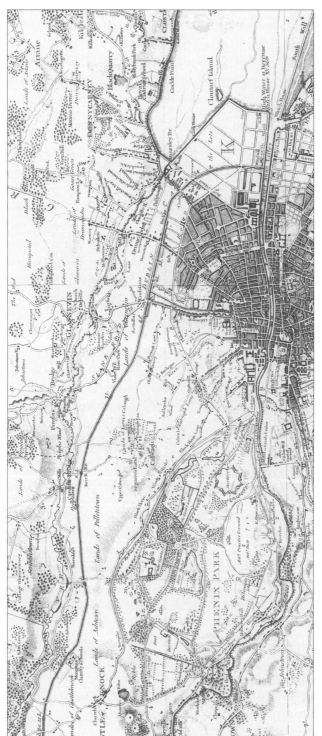

John Taylor's Map of the Environs of Dublin, 1816

Foreword

Now, you can take my word for it. You won't be able to hold a candle to this super, cool, magic book on Rathborne's candles and candle-making history. Holding candles to things when I was a chiseller was the measuring-stick between good, fair, bad and excellent. If you could not 'hold a candle' to it, it was excellent, a masterpiece, a work of art and craft, far above the best, and miles and miles from the tuppenny ha'penny place which was the opposite end of the candle.

Another favourite childhood saying was borrowed from the poet Rudyard Kipling. This saying was only conferred on someone who had done a great thing, like Bernard Neary, who has written a wonderful book called *The Candle Factory*. Now Bernard well deserves the Kipling words – 'You're a better man than I am, Gunga Din'.

This book takes you back three thousand years and more, and then on to the Hole in the Wall and Michael Collins; from the medieval Chester town to Crampton Court beside Dan Lowrey's Empire Palace, and on to the East Wall candle factory. I have always taken great pride in the fact that Dublin's oldest firm, Rathborne's, the tallow chandlers, made their products down the centuries, not only for the rich and the church, but for the poor as well:

> *A farthing candle to show you light*
> *To read the bible on a Saturday night.*

Well, I often had my farthing candle, but God forgive me, I wasn't reading the Bible, no, it was all those penny horribles with

Desperate Dan and Korky the Cat. A farthing was a quarter of an old penny, the smallest-value coin in Europe. When darkness falls all around with an ESB power-cut, what serves man and woman as light? What are the first words said? 'Where did you put those candles? Where's the butt end of the red Christmas candle?'

This book is their story, very well told by my friend Bernard Neary. Like the old candles, this book will last forever.

Is Mise,

Le mór mór meas,

ÉAMONN MAC THOMÁIS

Preface

It gives me great pleasure, as Managing Director of John G. Rathborne Ltd, to introduce this excellent book by local historian, Bernard Neary. Bernard has produced a detailed and informative account of the history of one of the world's oldest firms.

Rathborne's had just celebrated its half-millennium simultaneously with Dublin City's millennium when I was appointed manager in 1989. The sheer antiquity of the firm was overwhelming, and it was fascinating to supervise the production of candles from the modern, high-technology machinery installed by my immediate predecessors and also from a simple metal carousel, similar to that used for centuries. Within the industry there existed a mass market, satisfied by high-output machinery, side by side with a growing market for the handmade product. My challenge was to steer the company successfully as we all headed towards the year 2000.

The company has always been able to adapt and change, and this is probably why Rathborne's has been able to exist for over five hundred years. Soon the firm will have been trading during seven consecutive centuries. Change, however, has usually been gradual, and this is epitomised by both its long-serving personnel, several of whom have been with the company over forty years, and by the trust of its exceptionally loyal customers. Recent developments include the refurbishment of the factory façade and the establishment of a richly-stocked factory shop open to the public.

I would especially like to thank Bernard Neary, who has performed a labour of love. In recording our first five hundred years of business in Ireland, he has made the job of whoever writes the one-thousand-year history a much easier task. At a time when the humble candle has become an item of high fashion, I hope that this book, which was envisaged as a way of sharing Rathborne's long, unique history, will bring pleasure to all who read it.

PEADAR LENNON

Storeroom, Dunsinea, c.1896.

Acknowledgments

The author wishes to thank the following, without whose help this book would not have been possible: David Bedlow, Eileen Chambers, Mary Clarke, Simon Curran, Marjorie Daly, Mairéad Dunlevy, Brendan Faughnan, Peggy Horan, Bernard Hynes, Leonard Hynes, Peadar Lennon, Éamonn Mac Thomáis, Bridget McCaul, T. McCluskie, Hugh Eimer McCormick, Peter McCready, Christy Moran, Ray Moulton, The Big Pineapple, Lennon Neary, Tom O'Connor, Frank Pelly, Aidan Prior, Rose Marie and Joseph Rathborne, John Reid, Noel Sugg, Dr Vivion Tarrant, Theresa Treacher, Liam Wylie and Peter Young.

Finally, a special thanks to Colin O'Carroll of Irish Shell for his vision and enthusiasm, which has made this book possible, and to my two diligent proofreaders, Seamus Glackin and John O'Sullivan, for their time, advice and help.

(Photo Brendan Fogarty)

1998 Staff Picture:

Back Row: *Andrew Kneeshaw, Justin Kneeshaw, Joe Brennan, Derek Brady, Gavin Clarke, Terry Roche, Owen Foster; Carl Roche, David Buggy, Peadar Lennon, Michael Bell, Alan Patchell, Paul Flood, Eddie O'Connor; Bobby Leppla, Joe Byrne, John Smith, Liam Connolly, Joe Quaile, Michael Duffy*

Front Row: *Betty Byrne, Monica Stewart, Lorna Rooney, Ann Gaughan, Joan Cunningham, Patricia Mulhall, Catherine Delaney, Jacinta O'Reilly, Janet Gray, Marie Tully, Geraldine Quaile, Joanne Fennessy, Karen Fox*

CHAPTER ONE

Brief History of Candle-Making

Candlelight was one of man's oldest answers to the problem of supplying light in dark. Evidence of this fact is shown by candlesticks from Egypt and Crete, the cradles of civilisation, dating to at least 3000 BC. Candelabra were among the artefacts discovered in the ancient ruins of Pompeii, the city buried under a thick layer of ash and lava by the eruption of Mount Vesuvius in 79 AD, and it is also in that century that we find the first recorded description of the candle, in the writings of Pliny the Younger. He described candles made from threads of flax coated with pitch and wax, and also mentioned rush-lights made from rush peeled on one side and dipped into melted fat or wax, used for making funeral lights. Roman candle-makers produced one form of candle by a method still in use today. The candle was made of tallow, or of beeswax cleaned with sea water and bleached by exposure to the sun. The wick was made of a roll of papyrus impregnated with sulphur, and the candle was built up by repeated dipping in the melted tallow or wax. Nowadays candles made in this way are called *dips* to distinguish them from candles made in moulds – and though beeswax is still a raw material wicks are no longer, naturally, made from papyrus.

In Ireland the history of candlelight is closely related to the history of one of the oldest firms in the world, that of John G. Rathborne Limited. Rathborne's, which started production in

Dublin's Winetavern Street in the 1480s and is still making candles in their factory on Dublin's East Wall Road, have been in continuous production for over five hundred years.

The word candle (from *candeo*, to shine) was introduced into the English language as an ecclesiastical term, probably as early as the eighth century AD. It was known in classical times and denoted any kind of taper made of wax or animal fat enclosing a fibrous wick for the purpose of giving light. It is doubtful if the use of candles in medieval times spread far beyond the great halls, churches, castles and monasteries occupied by the religious and the very highest in society. Originally a home industry like weaving, by the early thirteenth century candle-making had become a craft and despite limited markets for the product it was a thriving business to be associated with. In a Paris tax-list of 1292, seventy-one chandlers are mentioned.

The quality of the light emitted depended on the candle material – for example, beeswax burned brighter than tallow. It was not until the sixteenth century – a period of remarkable elevation in the living standards of ordinary people – that the use of candles started to become widespread. The evidence of the use of candles increases from this time and candlesticks appear regularly in household inventories from the early 1500s.

For the masses who could not afford candles, the most common form of lighting was the rush-light, made by drawing a rush through waste kitchen fat. In 1763 John Aubrey, the antiquarian, reported that the inhabitants of Ockley in Surrey made their own rush-lights. Rush-lights continued in use in England until late in the nineteenth century, and in Wales the tradition lingered on into the mid-twentieth century. The tradition waned in Ireland during the early 1800s, when people could not afford meat to produce the waste kitchen fat used to make rush-lights. Another form of candle was made in Ireland by rolling soft resin around a linen rag; these were called snobs. Yet another type of candle in use in this country was made from strips of bog wood or fir, which is sometimes known as candle wood. Rush-candles were made in the same way as rush-lights, but were dipped many times in fat until they assumed the required size, whereas the rush-light was only thinly cased with fat. During the Emergency, the war years in the 1940s, many people in Ireland, particularly in the west, were forced to return to making rush-lights to provide light when supplies of candles and oil were severely reduced.

The renowned Gaelic writer, Tomás Ó Crothán, who was born on the Great Blasket (or the Western Isle) in 1856, recalls the use of rush-lights in his book *An t-Oileánach*:

> Cressets and fish-oil, with tapers or rushes on the cresset, renewed as they burnt away – that's the first contrivance for making light that I knew. The fish-oil was got from scad and pollock. 'Dip' was the name we gave to the scad's fat; the pollock's grease was called 'liver'. We used to melt it. They employed seal-oil for light too, but they didn't put much of that in the cressets, for they used to gulp it down themselves, dipping their bread of Indian meal in it, and they needed it badly enough. I was well in the teens, I think, while this kind of light was still in use. The cresset was a little vessel, shaped like a boat or canoe, with one or two pointed ends, three or four feet to it, and a little handle or grip sticking out of its side – the whole thing was about eight or ten inches long. The fish-oil was put into it, the reed or wick was dipped in the oil and passed over the pointed end of the cresset and as it burnt away it was pushed out. The pith of the rush formed the wick, and they often used a soft twine of cotton or linen for it. They would often use a large shell instead of a cresset for a light. I don't remember at what date paraffin came into use. A fragment of turf or a chip of bog-deal was the older fashion, I used to hear them say.

Of course, in good times the islanders burned candles, and in 1878 – a year of plenty on the Western Isle – their purchases from the town of Dingle included candles; Rathborne's dispatch records from the Essex Street office for this year show a railway dispatch invoice to Tralee, from where the consignment of candles was

delivered to Dingle by horse-drawn transport. By the time
Ó Crothán died in 1937 it was the tilly lamp that provided the main
source of light on the island.

The form of lighting mentioned in *An t-Oileánach* was preferred
in coastal areas, and generally a fish-oil lamp was used in localities
where such oil was easily available. It was commonly found on the
Antrim coast and on Rathlin Island, where the lamp was called the
crusie. The crusie lamp was adapted for burning a loose wick,
supported as nearly horizontal as possible, as animal and vegetable
oils are much more sluggish than mineral oils in response to
capillary attraction. Each lamp consisted of an upper and lower pan
with projecting lips. The wick was placed in the upper pan, which
was supported on a ratchet projection set obliquely on the upright
of the lower pan and arranged so that the lower pan caught the
overflow of oil. The upright at the top was bent at right angles to
bring the end over the centre of gravity and through it a hook
passed for suspension. Hooks were made by hammering red-hot
iron into moulds; samples are on exhibit in the Ulster Museum.

The early settlers in America first made their candles from deer
fat or from the wax of wild bees. Later they discovered how to
produce a green wax by boiling the berries of the bayberry tree, a
species of myrtle native to the country. In China the material used

Candlenut tree, Queensland
(PHOTO BERNARD NEARY)

was insect wax, which was a
lustrous white deposit left by a
small insect called the *loccus pela*
on the branches of trees. Apart
from simple processes like
bleaching or boiling, practically
all these materials were used in
their natural state. In Australia,
the first white settlers lit up
their darkness by making use of
the candlenut tree to produce
their candles. Some varieties of
the candlenut yield an oil which
was used to make candles in the

early days of white settlement and it was later used in oil-based paints and varnishes, explaining the candlenut's alternative name of *varnish tree*. The trees' nuts, pushed onto a bamboo splint, will burn like a candle. In tropical Australia the candlenut is a common shade tree. Frequently, owners of the tree discover that the nut tastes like the macadamia nut and may be processed in a similar manner; in Papua New Guinea and nearby islands the nut is commonly ground up and used in prepared dishes.

In the nineteenth century a French chemist, Michel Eugene Cheveral, separated the fatty acid from the glycerin of fat to produce stearic acid, from which superior candles could be made; further processes for production appeared in rapid succession during that century. In addition to stearin, two other important sources were discovered: spermaceti, taken from the head cavity of the sperm whale, and paraffin wax, derived from petroleum. A composite of paraffin wax and stearic acid became the basic candle ingredient by the turn of the present century.

Candle Wicks and Snuffers

The development of the wick has been of paramount importance in the long history of candles. The early tallow dips or tapers contained a rush wick that was peeled except for a strip on one side. The portion of the rush in the flame curved, with the strip of peel inside the curve, so that the tip of the rush was always in the hot outer mantle of the flame and burnt away cleanly. The early twisted cotton candlewick behaved differently. It stood bolt upright in the cool interior of the flame so that a head of black soot formed on its end. This resulted in a dim light and smoky burning that called for frequent snuffing, which was done with snuffers. Snuffers were probably introduced here from Italy during the fifteenth century and continued in use until the

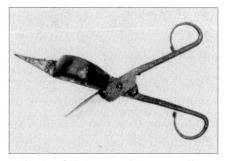

A pair of plain wrought-iron snuffers. Similar examples were made in brass.

invention of the plaited wick, which dispensed with their services. Snuffers were made of iron, brass and pewter, though some of the better kinds were made in Sheffield plate and silver and were usually accompanied by trays of the same material. Both snuffers and trays offered a fine field for the ingenuity of the makers and frequently show elaborate ornamentation. Hobday's snuffers, as specified in his patent of 1818, were, in common with most mechanical types, made of polished steel. Others were made of plain wrought-iron and brass. The practical part of the snuffer is the box with its hinged lid and a hidden spring that kept the snuffer closed after use, and so prevented the fumes of the snuffed wick from escaping into the air of the room. Douters, not to be confused with snuffers, extinguished the flame by nipping the wick.

A candle with a wick so constructed as to require no snuffing engaged the ingenuity of practical men until 1820, when another Frenchman, Cambraceres, discovered that if cotton were plaited instead of being twisted the wick would behave just like the peeled rush in rush-lights. A regular clean-burning wick which required no snuffing was thus invented. That century also saw the rapid development of candle-making equipment, the most significant invention being a machine consisting of rows of moulds in a metal tank that is alternately heated and cooled. After the moulds are cooled, pistons eject the candles. Spools of wicking from the bottom of the machine are threaded through the pistons to pass through the candle mould. As the cooled candles are ejected, the wicks are cut. Such machines, in pristine condition and perfect working order, are still in use today in Rathborne's candle factory on Dublin's East Wall Road.

Candle and Rush-Light Holders

The candle spawned a whole industry in the area of candle-holder manufacture, in which Irish craftsmen excelled. Silver candlesticks were made in Ireland from the late seventeenth century onwards. The more usual shapes were those of the Corinthian pillar or column or the balustrade. A more unusual type was of tripod form. Candlesticks were also made from iron, brass and glass. Chandeliers and crystal glass candlesticks have, through the years and right up to the present day, allowed craftsmen to produce fine examples of their trade – one has only to see a Waterford Crystal cut-glass candlestick to appreciate the skill involved. One of the first examples of Irish glass candlesticks was produced, probably around 1675, by Captain Philip Roche, who took up the trade at the insistence of Thomas Woulfe, his brother-in-law. According to an article on the history of the industry in the *Dublin Chronicle* of 11 September 1788, Captain Roche built and ran an 'extensive and convenient flint glass candle-stick works' at St Mary's Lane, Dublin. These works were directly opposite a plot of ground owned by Joseph Rathborne, which he later left in his will to his son, William, so it is possible that Captain Roche's business and that of Rathborne's were complementary to each other.

Rush-lights were also used in holders; the earliest forms of holder were made of wood but later examples were made in iron, usually wrought but sometimes cast. Some of them were made for

Left to right: *Irish silver candlestick by Robert Calderwood, c.1745, 11 inches in height; Irish silver candlestick, probably by John Segar, 1685-7, 6 inches in height; Irish silver candlestick, maker unknown, c.1745, 10 inches in height.*

(PHOTO COURTESY OF NATIONAL MUSEUM)

particular use in trades, others to stand upon the table, and still others were in the form of floor standards. The rush was held obliquely between a pair of pincer-like nippers – a position impossible in the case of candles – and consequently required no snuffing. A counterbalance weight frequently terminated in a knob or curl, and when rush-candles came into vogue the counterbalance was formed into a candle socket, which was provided in the standard varieties, with a spring adjustment to raise or lower the light upon the upright shaft, the curved line of the spring often giving an ornamental result. Sometimes the adjustment was done with a wooden ratchet and loop. A great number of such holders were made in Ulster during the eighteenth and early nineteenth centuries, and a fine collection of rush-light and candle holders is held by the Ulster Museum.

Candle Moulds

The invention of the candle mould is attributed to Sieur de Brez, a French nobleman of the fifteenth century. Sieur de Brez was reputed to have been a very gay courtier who was an able soldier and statesman and also Chamberlain to Charles VII. The importance of candlelight at court functions may to some extent account for the interest of such a man in domestic problems. His invention, which was introduced into Ireland at the beginning of the sixteenth century and which remained in use for hundreds of years, was a wooden frame having one or more metal tubes set into it and some simple device for holding the wicks stretched through the centres of the moulds. The mould was slightly conical to allow the candle to be readily drawn out when hardened. A mould of this type is still in use in Rathborne's factory for making candles of special shapes and sizes, and there are still a few examples of old moulds that were in use in this country until relatively recent times.

The first notable improvement over the moulds of Sieur de Brez was made by an Englishman, Thomas Binns of Marylebone, in a patent in 1801. He was a maker of domestic water flushes and his invention concerned the water-cooling of candle moulds. These he fixed into a metal box into which cold water could be run, with an arrangement by which steam could be let into the water before the molten wax was poured in so that the wax was not chilled too rapidly. Besides giving faster production this method imparted a fine glossy finish to the candles. In 1834 Joseph Morgan of Manchester patented a machine which introduced the moveable piston, enabling the candles to be easily removed from the moulds. This invention facilitated continuous wicking, since the action of moving the pistons to eject the candles could be used to introduce fresh lengths of wick into the moulds. In the 1840s two Londoners, Joseph Tuck and William Palmer, invented a clamp for holding the candles after their release from the moulds and a mechanism for simultaneously ejecting all the candles from the moulds. Although these and other improvements were the inventions of Englishmen, their incorporation into the prototype of the modern-day candle machine was due to two Americans, John Stainthrop and Willis Humiston, who independently obtained patents in 1855.

The Demise of the Functional Candle

The introduction of gas lighting only dented the market for candlelight, as initially it was only installed in the homes of the wealthy or the artisan classes. Even after the introduction of the Gas Light Act for Dublin in 1821 the candle market remained buoyant and the industry was still a major provider of light outside the capital. It was the introduction of electricity that brought about the demise of the candle as an important light source. First the major cities were electrified – in 1898 Dublin Corporation accepted tenders totalling £20,000 for the cabling of Dublin city for public electric lighting by the Callender Cable & Construction Company and other firms – resulting in more and more businesses leaving the candle manufacturing industry. With the commencement of the ESB's Rural Electrification Scheme in 1946, the market for candles diminished radically. In a special RTÉ *Late Late Show* at the end of 1996 to commemorate the fiftieth anniversary of the introduction of the Scheme, one woman recalled turning on the electric light in order to ignite her candles and then switching it off again. After reigning supreme as the provider of light during darkness for over 3000 years the candle was finally eclipsed by the electric light.

In the UK the consumption of candles fell from 45,000 tons per annum in 1916 to an average of around 40,000 tons during the years from 1919 to 1931. By 1937 annual candle production had fallen to 25,000 tons, and by 1946 the annual output had fallen to 18,000 tons; thereafter it fell steadily until it reached 7000 tons in 1959. In Ireland the number of chandlers listed in *Thom's Directory* for the city of Dublin in 1868 was ninety-eight; by 1917 this was down to thirty-five; in 1935 the number of chandlers for the whole country numbered just thirteen. Further pressure was put on firms in Western Europe, including Rathborne's, when third-world countries started to establish their own indigenous candle industries. However, the trade survived and even as late as 1950 nearly five hundred people were directly employed in the Irish candle industry. In that year Rathborne's produced forty-five million household candles and still supplied the Irish mines, where miners' shifts were measured by the candle. The use of the candle as a prime source of light diminished considerably with the dramatic improvement in living standards after the Second World War. However, as peoples' living conditions improved rapidly in the late 1950s and early 1960s, there was a renaissance for the candle, which made a dramatic comeback as a decorative object and as a way of creating atmosphere. One has only to look at the candle display in any supermarket, craft shop or market stall to see that there is indeed a thriving market for the humble candle.

Traditions and Customs

For countless years it has been an Irish tradition that a lighted candle is placed at a window on Christmas Eve night. The candles, of various colours and in large half- or one-pound sizes, are left to burn all night and the underlying message is that anyone seeking shelter would know they were welcome there. The origin of the custom is forgotten, but remembering that the stable in Bethlehem was shown to the three wise men by a star in the sky, it can probably be   assumed   that   the   reason   for   lighting   candles   was   to commemorate that first Christmas Eve. Up to the early 1960s, in conjunction with this custom, many people also left a meal set for any weary late-night traveller on Christmas Eve, to show that the welcome which would be so readily given to Jesus was also extended to anyone else, however humble, if they were in need. The tradition of placing a candle in the window for all to see was very strong in Cabra West, Dublin, where the author grew up during the 1950s. Though sadly the practice has waned, despite the multiple variety of electric displays, including electric candles, for Christmas decorative purposes, the old tradition still survives. A walk along Croaghpatrick, Screen, Ardpatrick, Nephin, Ratoath, Broomebridge, Killala and Kilkieran Roads in Dublin 7 at 11 p.m. on Christmas Eve night 1995 was made magical by lighted candles burning brightly in the windows of thirty-seven houses.

With regard to the colour of the Christmas candle, each district had its own taste. For example in Limerick city and County Clare white candles were mainly used, in Bantry it was red, in the midlands it was pink and elsewhere red and green candles were popular. In some parts of Dublin the preferred colour was blue, though red dominated the capital. In Killarney nothing less than a one-pound candle generally sufficed for the occasion. In County Monaghan the white candle was burned until the late 1930s to early 1940s, when the red candle came into vogue. 'This was as a result of more and more people becoming able to afford the coloured one, which cost more than the plain white candle,' recalls Bernadette Brady from Killykespin.

Another tradition was for shopkeepers to give out candles to their customers at Christmas time. Anyone who remembers pre-supermarket Dublin will recall the big red Rathborne Christmas candle which the grocer placed on the counter and rolled up in a sheet of brown paper in such a way that no sellotape or twine was required. It was then presented to the customer with a hearty 'Happy Christmas'. James Tully from Keady, Co. Roscommon, recalls Christmas time in that quiet village:

> When I was growing up in the village, before the Emergency, the grocer gave his favoured customer a

candle, a Christmas cake and a bottle of wine. The candle was always a red Rathborne one and on Christmas night, walking up the Boyle road, we would see the side of Arigna mountain dotted with flickering lights. When I entered the grocery trade in Cabra West, Dublin, in 1956, the red Rathborne was still given out as a present to regular customers. I continued that practice, and right up to my retirement from the trade in 1989 I gave out red Rathbornes to all my regular customers. Even today I still give out an odd packet of Rathborne candles to some old customers of mine when I meet them in Cabra West at Christmas time.

P.J. McCaffrey (left) *presenting red Rathbornes to Agnes Kelly and Dermot Byrne, Christmas 1996.*

The custom waned with the opening of cut-price stores, the forerunner to the big supermarkets. With new stores like the Big Bear in Talbot Street gaining an ever-increasing share of the retail food trade, the practice died away in many parts of the country. However, the custom survives today and during recent Christmases it was appropriate to see the proprietors of the Hole in the Wall public house giving out red Rathbornes to their customers, as this historic pub is situated near the old Rathborne plant at Dunsinea, on the stretch of Blackhorse Avenue from where the firm once drew much of its work force. Indeed, the Dodd and Daly familys, for generations employed in the candle factory at Dunsinea, are still represented on the avenue, just a stone's throw away from the pub. The present owners of the Hole in the Wall, P.J. McCaffrey and his wife Margaret, have a keen sense of history, which is obvious from even a brief visit to their hostelry. In the time of John G. Rathborne it was Michael Kennedy, a land steward living in Springfield Lodge, which was then situated off Blackhorse Avenue, adjacent to present-day Screen Road, who called time. When Henry B. was running the candle factory, the pub's proprietor was Levinus Doyle. He renamed the premises, calling it the Blackhorse Tavern, and died during the same year that Henry retired from the candle trade, in April 1915. It is worth noting that Levinus Doyle's widow, Catherine, continued to run the pub until 1943. The use of candlelight as an atmosphere-enhancer in this famous Dublin pub is a long-time practice of the current proprietors, who are most generous in the amount of candlelight that they provide. They purchase all of their supplies from Rathborne's.

A custom common in the west of Ireland was the lighting of twelve small, coloured candles on the night of the Epiphany. Tommy Kenny from Ballinasloe in County Galway recalls:

> On the twelfth night, the 5th January, we had twelve candles and you put your name on a candle and you knelt down and said the Rosary, and the *piseog* – superstition – was that whoever's candle went out first was going to die. One lad's candle would go out horrid quick and the thing was that every year it was a different person. Sure I remember crying at home, 'I don't want to die, I don't want to die.' We used to use little Rathborne candles. But during the Second World War you couldn't get them type of candles and the parents would cut the big red ones and I'll never forget it – they only had little bits of the big candle and we were all night waiting for them to burn out. We had more Rosaries said by the time they went out.

In Limerick the large candles were also burned on All Souls' Night, 2 November. Still another curious custom in County Wicklow, practised in living memory, was to treat pigs with tallow dips mixed with herbs to cure some form of swine fever similar to foot-and-mouth disease. These home-made candles were also used for curing constipation in pigs.

Easter Rituals

In the Jewish faith and in the Christian church the use of candles is widespread. In the Christian faith a multitude of candles and lamps used in the ceremonies at Easter-tide is an ancient custom which the first Christian Emperor Constantine followed in Constantinople in the fourth century. It is true that candles, like incense and lustral water, were commonly employed in pagan worship and in the rites paid to the dead; but from a very early period the Christian church took them into her service. The symbolism of the candles accepted by the Catholic Church is that the wick symbolises the soul of Christ, the wax the body and the flame the divinity which absorbs and dominates both. Thus the great Paschal candle represents Christ and the smaller candles each individual Christian who strives to reproduce Christ in life. The grains of incense inserted into the Paschal candle symbolised the spices which the holy women brought to embalm the body of Christ. The mystery of the Trinity is symbolised by the triple candle. It is said that the three candles were joined together in the form of the reed so that when lighted together they would not be easily extinguished during the procession for the Vigil Office. Candles for liturgical purposes should be of beeswax; the reason for this is based on the theory of the supposed virginity of bees. Though church attendance has declined in Ireland over the past twenty years, the demand for candles at Easter time is still very high, keeping the candle-makers busy as the Paschal candle is a handmade product.

Candles have for centuries held ritualistic symbolism in cultures throughout the world. A curious medieval practice was that of offering at any favoured shrine a candle or a number of candles equalling in measurement the height of the person for whom some favour was being requested. This was called 'measuring to' whatever saint was petitioned, and the practice in turn gave its name to the term 'measuring up to'. The practice can be traced back to the time of St Radigund (587 AD) and survived through the Middle Ages; it was especially common in England and western France during the twelfth and thirteenth centuries.

In Sweden the great Advent festival is St Lucy's Day (in honour of

Wax bleaching fields, Dunsinea, c.1896. Note man in centre of picture.

the saint who was martyred for her faith in the fourth century AD) on 13 December. Called Little Yule, it is connected with the ancient winter festival and the lighting of fires and candles to celebrate the return of light, warmth and sun. In every Swedish village there was a Lucia Queen – a young girl dressed in white with a crown of lighted candles on her head. She had to get up early in the morning and bring coffee and food to the farmhouses in the area; she also had to visit animal sheds and stables. She was accompanied by a man on horseback and a procession of young people carrying lighted candles and dressed as maids of honour, Biblical characters, trolls and demons, representing the triumph of good over evil, the return of the sun's power and the defeat of darkness. The Lucia Queen symbolized the coming of light and prosperity to all humans and animals alike.

Even the colourful and majestic tradition of the Christmas tree involves the use of candles. The Christmas tree originally came from Germany, where in the eighth century AD a Father Boniface was trying to convert the people to Christianity. On finding out that the tree was their god, he became very angry and seizing an axe he cut a tree down, whereupon a tiny fir tree sprang up in its place. The fir is known as the tree of Christ with its evergreen leaves pointing up to heaven, and the tradition of putting lighted candles on the Christmas tree is still practised in parts of Germany to this day. During the Reformation, Martin Luther used a candlelit tree as an image of the starlit heavens from where Christ had come.

The Candle as Symbol of Hope

The candle can be a powerful symbol. An example of this is the Amnesty International logo, which shows a candle wrapped in barbed wire. The Amnesty symbol is familiar world-wide and it stirs up powerful feelings within human hearts. People working for peace often hold candlelit demonstrations. In 1996, when the people of East Timor held candlelit vigils to commemorate the brutal 1992 murder of peaceful demonstrators in Santa Cruz cemetery, Dili, by the repressive Indonesian occupiers, Senator David Norris and Patricia McKenna MEP tried to attend the demonstration, but were stopped by the Indonesians in Bali while *en route* to Dili. Candles smuggled to them in Bali from East Timor were lit on their return at a ceremony in Ireland. Rathborne's supplied a large consignment of candles, at very favourable rates, to the East Timor Ireland Solidarity Campaign, for use in a huge candlelit demonstration in Dublin during the visit to Ireland of the Australian Premier, Paul Keating, in 1994.

The candle is also a symbol of inspiration. For Dr Karl Konig, the founder of the world-wide Camphill movement which caters for children and adults with special needs, the candle was to become a powerful symbol. On Advent Sunday in 1927, at the Steiner-instituted School of Spiritual Science in Dornach, Switzerland, he went into the Advent Garden and saw handicapped children walking with lighted candles in a special festival. He wrote afterwards:

> In this hour the decision was taken that I would dedicate my life to the care and education of these children. It was a promise I gave to myself: to build a hill upon which a big candle was to burn that so many infirm and handicapped children would be able to find their way to this beacon of hope and to light their own candles so that each single flame would be able to radiate and shine forth.

Dr Konig later fled Nazi Austria in 1939 and in the loneliness of a tiny room in a wartime London back-street, he stared at a lighted candle on the mantelpiece: 'The small candle in front of me lit the few green branches on the mantelpiece and the gas fire hummed a low song. The flame of the candle jerked and quivered and threw strange shadows on the wall. I had left Europe behind me. The language is foreign, the people strangers.' As he thought of his future in his new country, he wondered what he would do and thought of his wife, who was about to join him in London. In the flickering candlelight he turned his eyes to an English bible: 'The light of the candle now was quiet and bright and my eyes turned to a small book which a kind person had given me as a Christmas present.' Looking at the candle he thought deeply, and then understood his thoughts. The following year Karl Konig, together with his wife Tilla Maasberg and a small band of Austrian refugees, moved into a small house on a twenty-five-acre estate seven miles from Aberdeen, in the north-east of Scotland, and commenced their own brand of care for the mentally handicapped. Despite terrible obstacles in the path of Karl Konig and his supporters, including a period of internment as enemy aliens, the Camphill Movement took root and grew and is now active throughout the world, including Ireland.

In the ancient world candles were used by peoples in times of war as symbols of hope and protection; in some African cultures they were used for casting both good and evil spells. An interesting book by Henri Gamache, published in New York in 1942 and titled *The Master Book of Candle Burning*, covers all aspects of the rituals of candle burning, including the use of coloured candles in such rituals.

For 2000 or more years the candle has been the most vivid of religious symbols. However, candles are not only a feature of church services, the companion of altars and chancels and processions. As traditional Jewish family ceremonies teach us, they can carry their symbolism into our own homes, at our meal tables and even in private prayer at home. The loving couple, young or older, dining by candlelight at home or in a restaurant, or the domestic host/hostess arranging the candelabra on the dinner-party table, are probably (perhaps intuitively) aware of this symbolism. The so-called 'Father of Electricity', Michael Faraday, was deeply aware of the powerful symbolism of the candle. One of his most famous and successful lectures, originally given to children in 1848 and later published as a book, was the six-part *The Chemical History of a Candle*. In the lectures, aided by some particularly spectacular demonstrations, he covered almost the whole range of scientific knowledge at the time. Michael Faraday closed his lectures with the following words:

> What wonders cluster round a candle, what strange and powerful knowledge becomes ours as we trace out and consider its powers. What instruments of good (and of evil) are thus placed in our hands, and what an open door it offers to us in the wisdom of God in the creation.

Factory workshop, Dunsinea, c.1896.

CHAPTER TWO

Five Hundred Years A-Growing

There are a number of theories regarding the coming to Ireland of the Rathborne family and their subsequent establishing of a candle-manufacturing business in 1488. The name of Rathborne has many variants: Rathbone, Rabone, Rathbun, Radbone, Raybone, Rawbone, Rathborn and Rathburne. The exact origins of the surname are uncertain: it might be English, meaning 'of Ruabon', or it may be from the Welsh 'Rhathbon', meaning 'stumpy clearing or plain' and referring to an original owner who lived in such a place. The Irish name for Rathborne derived from the old Gaelic word 'Rathbone', meaning 'white fort', after an original owner of such a home.

According to the Rathborne genealogical tree the family name can be traced back to a John Rathborne who came from one of the northern shires of Wales and settled around the year 1265 in the Hundred of Macclesfield, East Cheshire, where he obtained a grant of land from Henry III at Masefen, Malpas. He married a lady by the name of Gwenaileane and they had a son, William Rathbone, who also obtained land in Cheshire from Edward I (Edward Longshanks), who reigned from 1272 to 1307. William's sons, Philip and John, also lived in Cheshire; Philip acquired lands at Hampton in 1316 and John was granted lands at Tussyncham, Malpas, by Charter dated at Eaton in 1316. John's son, Henry Rathbone, was living at Masefen in the seventh year of Richard II,

1385. The Rathborne family motto was *Suaviter et Fortiter* – Mildly and Firmly. This family and their descendants lived in and around the City of Chester for generations and they obviously enjoyed prosperous livelihoods, for they held many public positions, becoming city sheriffs and aldermen. One John Rathbone was Sheriff of Chester in 1503 and Mayor in 1514; Richard Rathbone was Sheriff in 1582 – this name is spelt Raybone in the *History of Chester* – then Alderman from 1590 to 1598 and finally Mayor in 1598–9.

There are many early references of the name linking it to Chester: a Peter Radbone of Chester married Elizabeth Smyth of London in 1547 (Marriage Licences, London); in 1604 Thomas Rawbone married Alice Ohes in Chester (Register of Prestbury Church); and in 1605 the will of Anne Rathbone of Martan, Cheshire, was read in Chester. It was from this branch of the family then that the first Rathborne came to Ireland.

In Ireland the surname was found mostly in counties Leitrim and Cavan but the family have been represented in other districts around the country. Ruby and Ann Rathborne lived in Macetown, County Meath, for many years; indeed there are a number of families bearing the name Rathborne living in Meath. Rose Marie and Joseph Rathborne live in the rural area of Macetown and their family live in the surrounding countryside. They can trace their origins back to Joseph and Mary Anne Rathborne, who were both born in 1785 at Ballymore, County Galway. The name was present in Dublin city and in St Margaret's in County Dublin, Mullagh and Kells in County Cavan, and in County Fermanagh. John and Joseph Rathborne, whose Christian names are common among the long line of Rathborne chandlers, ran a corn mill and farm at Skearke, in the parish of Moynalty, County Cavan, in the early 1900s. There is a bridge called Rathborne's Bridge on the Cavan-Monaghan border.

There have been many distinguished members of the Rathborne clan. William Rathborne, born in Loughrea, County Galway, on 16 July 1748, entered the British Navy in 1763 as an able seaman on the *Niger* with Sir Thomas Adams, based on the Newfoundland Station. In 1792 he was appointed captain and on 14 March 1795 served in the reduction of Corsica, where he was wounded in the eye and arm; he was later made a naval commander on 9 November 1795. Retiring in 1810 on a British Government pension of £300 per annum, in 1815 he was nominated a CBE. He died in 1831. A Captain Anthony Blake Rathborne submitted documents to the British Government defending Lieutenant-General Charles J. Napier's governance of Scinde in 1854, and in 1898 one Ambrose B. Rathborne wrote a book on his fifteen years pioneering in the native states of the Malay peninsula, entitled *Camping and Tramping in Malaya*. Julian Rathbone was a Dorset-based author who wrote *The Last English King*. The actor Sir Basil Rathbone was born in Johannesburg in 1892 and began his working life in Liverpool in the insurance industry. He first worked on the stage in the UK with the Frank Benson Company and in 1912 he toured the USA, performing Shakespeare. He saw service in the First World War with the Liverpool & Scottish Regiment. He went to the USA after the war and became a prominent film actor, taking part in both American and English productions, but from 1939 he worked almost exclusively with Universal Studios. He starred in *The Adventures of Robin Hood* in 1938. He died in 1967.

The most popular theory is that the original Rathborne branch that set up the candle-making business in Dublin fled Chester due to political persecution, having supported the House of York against the House of Lancaster in the Wars of the Roses of 1455–85. A more likely explanation is that the migration of some members of the Rathborne family was a commercial decision – the River Dee was silting up and the candle-manufacturing Rathbornes based on its Chester banks were facing a crisis with regard to their thriving markets. They found themselves forced to relocate or go out of business.

In those days the port of Liverpool was just a handful of hovels beside the Mersey pool and Chester was a bustling, busy port, whose large fleets traded with many English and European cities including Dublin. Consequently there were strong links between the ancient City of Chester and Dublin. Erlington Ball, in his article 'Communication between London and Dublin from the Thirteenth

Century', notes that 'Chester was always in direct communication with Dublin from a very early period'. Indeed, all through the Middle Ages, Chester was the centre of trade between Great Britain and Ireland. As the port went into decline due to the silting-up of the River Dee, the Rathborne family chose Dublin as the base for a new manufacturing enterprise. It is probable that the family was engaged in the craft of candle-making at Chester from the early 1400s, and it is also probable that they were members of the guild of Barber Surgeons. This company is known to have been in existence by the year 1475 and was granted charters by the Mayor of Chester in 1540 and by King Edward VI in 1550. It combined the crafts of medicine, hair-trimming and candle-making and it met in local inns and at the Phoenix Tower in Chester (which later became known as King Charles Tower).

William Rathborne came to Ireland in the 1450s, and his name is the first record of the Rathbornes in Dublin, appearing as William Rabowe in the *Dublin Assembly Rolls* for the year 1455. As the traditional founding date for the Rathborne candle-making business is 1488, it is probable that it was his son, John, who established and nurtured the tallow chandlery in the busy Christchurch area of Dublin city, in Wyne Tavern (now called Winetavern) Street, and there are existing title deeds showing him as having property in that area. It is also possible that William Rathborne or Rabowe brought over his tools and skills of the trade and set up a chandlery in Dublin to pass on to his son. In any event the business took hold and during the early 1500s it thrived under the capable stewardship of John Rathborne. The Rathbornes chose an ideal location for their business as the main concentration of population in Dublin city was then in the Christchurch area. Part of the quays were reclaimed by the dumping of city rubbish and this allowed for deeper berthage at Wood Quay, which was the main area for shipping imports and exports in the 1400s and 1500s. Finally – and very importantly – Garrett Mor Fitzgerald, the Great Earl of Kildare, was at the peak of his power, ensuring a stable political climate for the economy to prosper.

Dublin at the time was a walled city, very compact and safely – or intimidatingly, depending on your point of view – nestled in the shadows of Dublin Castle. The streets we know from that time include Castle Street, Fishamble Street, High Street, Skinners Row and Winetavern Street. These streets were associated with the trades and activities being carried on in the district. The street where the Rathborne's carried on candle-making was the focus of the liquor trade, hence the name Winetavern Street; Cook Street was the location of the city's eating houses; Fishamble Street the site of the fish market; and Ship (or Sheep) Street was where sheep were sold.

John and his heirs kept the business ticking over nicely during the sixteenth century and successive generations of the family continued the craft. Early leases show candle-making members of the family owning numerous houses and plots of land in Dublin in the 1500s. The chandlery prospered through the turmoil of the Nine Years' War, which culminated in the might of Elizabethan England crushing the bold Irish forces of Aodh O'Neill, Aodh O'Donnell and O'Sullivan Beare at Kinsale in 1601. Twenty years later the name John Rathborne appears in an old Parish Register as residing in Wyne Tavern Street. This is the first reference in Irish records of the modern form of the name.

There is an interesting letter in the Chester City Records Office dated 21 February 1573 from William Fitzwilliam of Dublin (the 'Black Fitzwilliam' in the ballad *Follow Me up to Carlow*, he became a Lord Deputy of Ireland). Addressed to the Mayor of Chester, it requests that his servant Richard Rabone, who was 'furbishing a ship with provisions for his master', be 'exempt from impressment into any other services'. Richard's cargo naturally included a consignment of candles!

Among the acts and ordinances at the Easter 1583 meeting of the Common Council of Guilds in Dublin was one granting a charter to the Company of Tallow Chandlers. Some years later the Common Council felt it necessary to intervene in the marketplace owing to the high prices charged in different crafts; candles, shoes and bread were the subject of complaints. The records of the Council read as follows:

> Whereas the Company of Tallowchalloners are complayned on for exceeding the pryce of 111d the pound of candles, contrary to the effect of theire chartor; it is agreed and ordered by the aucthorytie of this assembly that from henceforth the said Company of tallow-challoners shall sell and utter candles at 111d sterling the pound, and not exceed that pryce, upon payne of forfeight theire chartor; and upon complaynt of eny citizen agaynst them, or eny of them, the Mayor to see the former lawes and this order executed against the offenders.

It appears that the Council did not have any economic expertise, for at the same meeting they permitted the butchers to charge more for tallow – the main ingredient for the candle. In 1599 the Council decreed that 'the tallow chandlers and their successors shall from henceforth furnish this city at all times with a goode store of candles of all sorts and shall not exceed the pryce of 111d sterling the pound and that of goode stuffe'. In that same year the Lord Mayor of Chester was a Richard Rathbone, which helps to dispute the theory that the Rathbornes fled political persecution in England.

Prosperity continued for the Rathbornes, helped by their winning the contract to supply candle-lighting to the city streets of Dublin. As a result they sought a suitable site in which they could expand their operations. Their search brought them north of the Liffey, where they were to relocate and remain in business – first in Brittain Street, then Prussia Street, then Dunsinea in Castleknock and finally at the East Wall – right up to the present day.

North of the Liffey

The Rathborne family re-established their candle-making business on Dublin's north side, in the parish of St Michan, in the first years of the seventeenth century. A map of Dublin by John Speed in the year 1610 gives an idea of the extent of St Michan's parish then. The ancient parish extended from the River Liffey northwards to Little Cabragh and from the shores of Dublin Bay on the east to the boundary of the present-day Phoenix Park on the west. Parish records show that Joseph Rathborne, Chandler, carried on his business at the junction of Bull Lane and Pill Lane in close proximity to the tavern The Bunch of Grapes. If the household premises of the Rathborne family remained adjacent to the business premises – as was to be the pattern until the twentieth century – then the family moved to the north side sometime prior to 1636, for there is a record in the Public Records Office of a William Raburne of Stoneybatter having made a will in that year. As John Rathborne lived in Wyne Tavern Street in 1621 – he is listed as rated for Parish Cess in St John's parish, Dublin, on 25 February 1621 – then the family and business must have relocated to the north side sometime between that year and 1636. It could have been after 1632, as the same parish records state that Mary Rathborne and Thomas Johns were married 'this Februarie in the year 1632'. It is also possible that John Rathborne and his family kept in touch with their roots on the south side of the city. For example, the records of the parish of St John's mention that John Rathborne married Elizabeth Reynolds on 20 May 1655, giving the name John Rathborne as the groom's father.

The Oxmanstown/Stoneybatter area of Dublin was, by the early 1600s, a thriving district. The family were among the area's most prominent business people. Following their relocation various family members became freemen of Dublin City – quite a high honour. In the fifty years from 1651 to 1701 no fewer than six members of the Rathborne family were so honoured: Thomas, John, Willus, Hugo, Johes and Joseph, though of these only Joseph is recorded as a candle-maker.

An examination of St Michan's parish register shows that on '22nd February 1637 died Jane Rabone, Widdow'. Another record notes that the 'banes of matrimony were published three several Lord's dayes between Richard Rathburne and Jane Morris on 4th, 11th and 18th January 1656'. The following year the records show 'the banes of matrimony were published three severall Lord's dayes between James Rathborne and Elizabeth Dillon, viz. on the 5th April 1657 and on the 12th and 19th dayes of the same, 1657'. That same year a Sarah, wife of Peter Rathbone, plasterer, is also mentioned in the parish records. Around this time too a Margery

Rathborne married Hugh Gunn, a schoolmaster, 'in the North Isle
of this Church of St Michan's'. By the end of the seventeenth
century Oxmanstown had become Dublin's most fashionable suburb
and the parish of St Michan a very wealthy and influential one. Its
population had increased so rapidly that it was divided by Act 9 of
William III into three separate parishes, New St Michan's, St Mary's
and St Paul's, incorporated on 20 May 1697. In the burial register of
St Michan's from about 1668, names of pewholders are frequently
mentioned as coffins were, in numerous instances, laid beneath the
seats.

Around this time an item appears in the records of the Guilds of
Dublin which shows that the Corporation of Tallow Chandlers and
Soapboylers, having presented a petition to the authorities in the
year 1675, complained that 'persons not free of the corporation
daily intruded on the corporation and used the trade proper for the
brethren of the said corporation, contrary to the tenor of their
charter'. The matter was considered by the Common Council,
which ordered that 'the said charter should be enrolled in the city
records and that the Lord Mayor should take steps to prevent such
an intrusion in the future'. The Common Council of the Guilds was
always prepared to lend a ready ear to any lawful complaints of the
Guildsmen, including healthy commercial competition emanating
from non-members.

It is from around this time, from the year 1700 onwards, that the
records of the Rathborne family become more detailed. This was
when the property and business of Rathborne's Wax Chandlers was
inherited by Joseph Rathborne, who was living in Dublin around
the turn of that century. Joseph Rathborne was a direct descendant
of the same Rathborne family that had included so many of its
numbers among the ranks of the sheriffs and mayors of Chester. He
was born in Drogheda, County Louth, in 1679. His father was
Richard Rathborne, who was born in Chester in 1640 and came to
Ireland during the reign of Charles II. One of two sons, Richard
married Mary Howard and became Sheriff of Drogheda in 1686,
while his brother William moved to Liverpool, where he settled and
reared a family. Richard's father was Joseph Rathbone, and his

father was Richard Rathbone (or Rabone), Alderman of Chester 1590–8 and Mayor in 1598–9, who married Anne, daughter of Joseph Taylor, of Chester. The father of this Richard Rabone was William Rathbone, who died in 1542, and his father was John Rathbone (or Rathborn), a Sheriff of Chester in 1503 and Mayor in 1514–15 and 1519–20. It was an uncle of this John Rathbone who, during the mid-1400s, came to Dublin and set up the first Rathborne candle manufacturing enterprise on Winetavern Street.

Whether Joseph had previously conducted business in the candle trade is difficult to ascertain, but at the age of twenty-one he became heir to the business and with his wife Catherine, the daughter of a William Norman of Skill, Drogheda, he settled on Pill-lane, now Chancery Street. It was here that he secured and expanded the main centre of the Rathborne candle manufacturing business. At that time Pill-lane ran along present-day Chancery Street, past the Bridewell Garda Station and the Metropolitan District Courts, and continued along today's Hammond Lane. In September 1896 the name of this once-famous thoroughfare was changed to Chancery-street following a petition to the Paving Committee of Dublin Corporation from all but one of the residents in the lane. The name change was not welcomed by the City Engineer, Spencer Harty, who stated that 'the Pill is a very old historic name in Dublin, and it is a pity to have it wiped out now. If, however, the Committee so desire, there is no objection to Chancery-street.'

By now there was an established market for candles and the industry was quite an important one – so much so that in 1709 an Act of Parliament placed a tax on candles and in addition outlawed the manufacture of candles in the home, then a common practice in rural areas. Under Joseph's capable hand the firm prospered and in 1711, as 'Joseph Rathborne, Dublin Chandler', he obtained a ninety-nine-year lease on 'a plot of ground on the north side of Great Britain Street, in the Lordship of St Mary's Abbey, from one John Brock, Joiner'. On 25 February 1715 he leased from one Caleb Small, a Kevin Street merchant, 'a plot of ground on the East Side

of Drumcondra Lane for fifty-one years at £2.11.3d per annum.'
This plot was probably intended as a site for a private residence.

On the Move

The workshop and factory were to move again, in 1722, for in that
year 'John Kerr, Dublin gent, Robt Sisson, Dublin, Joiner, demised
to Joseph Rathborne, Dublin, Tallow-Chandler, a parcel of ground
and a slaughter house, together with a yard and scalding-house,
situated in Rickison's yard, Boot Lane, Dublin, lately in the
occupation of Margaret Rickison and then in the possession of
Joseph Rathborne to hold from 25 March 1722 for seventy-seven
years at £8.0.0d per annum.' The following year Joseph Rathborne
leased another plot of ground 'on the north side of St. Mary's Lane
with the brick house and two cabbins thereon' and here he built
'severall goode houses'. In 1727 another piece of land in
Drumcondra Lane was leased by Joseph for seventy-six years at £4
per annum, perhaps as a marriage gift for one of his daughters.

A diligent worker and successful businessman, Joseph died in
1738 at his home in St Mary's Abbey. He had carried on the business
of a tallow chandler in Dublin for over thirty years. On his death the
business premises were at the corner of Boot Lane and St Mary's
Abbey. He left behind him his wife Catherine and seven children:
Richard, born in 1703, who was educated at Trinity College, Dublin
(BA 1726, MA 1729), and married Mary, daughter of Captain
Jonathon Wilson, Royal Navy[*]; William, the second eldest, a
candle- maker by trade whose lineage controlled the Rathborne
candle manufacturing enterprise into the early years of the
twentieth century; Joseph, the youngest, of whom very little is
known; Mary, married to Philip Crampton[**] 'by licence on June ye

---

[*] They settled in Ballymore, Co. Galway; one of their sons was also called Richard and
    he married Bridget Firman, of Selby, Yorkshire, in 1774. They too settled in
    Ballymore, where their first son, also Richard, was born in 1775, becoming High
    Sheriff in 1815 and a Captain in the British Army's 9th Dragoons. Descendants of
    this branch of the Rathborne family lived in New Zealand in 1830, in New York and
    New Jersey in 1915, in Louisiana in the 1950s and in County Meath up to the
    present day.

[**] Crampton was an Alderman and afterwards became Lord Mayor of Dublin. Their
    grandson was Sir Philip Crampton, created a Baronet in 1839.

5th 1727'; Catherine, married to John Fitzpatrick of Drumcondra; Dorothy, married to Francis Gladwell, Dublin merchant; and Alice, married to John Marsden, a Dublin tallow chandler, on 4 September 1738.

In his will, proved in June 1738, Joseph left bequests to all his family. The will, which is reproduced here as an appendix in order to give the reader an insight into the personality of this remarkable man, makes specific references to the continuation of the family business and to the tools of the trade. As can be seen from the bequests, Joseph Rathborne, the youngest son of Joseph senior, had been left certain property, including the chandlery, subject to his taking up and following the candle trade for a period of ten years – otherwise the benefit of the leases and properties relating to the candle-manufacturing business were to be sold and the proceeds divided equally among his brothers and sisters. By a Deed Poll in 1738 the Reverend Richard Rathborne and his sister Catherine, 'in consideration of the affection which they bore Joseph', released their brother 'from all demands that they might make upon any part' of the fortune if the business were to be sold, and consented that Joseph follow any business he might think fit. Later in that same year the youngest daughter, Alice, and her husband, John Marsden, signed similar statements. Joseph, who never married, did not inherit the deep family interest in candle-making and accordingly handed over all the business relating to candles to his brother William, already mentioned, who was the second son of old Joseph and a wax chandler by trade. He had developed a reputation for hard work in his father's factory, and old Joseph had assisted his young son in setting up his own candle manufacturing business, which he did in 1732 when he erected a small workshop at the back of his home on Essex Street, Dublin. Three years after entering the candle trade, on 8 March 1735, William married by licence one Ann, the daughter of Robert Billing, a well-known Dublin jeweller of the time. They had three children, Joseph, Anne and William. He became a very successful chandler, and around 1740, in an expansion of the

44 Essex Street (note Crampton Court
nameplate over laneway).
(PHOTO BERNARD NEARY)

business, he leased premises on Cabragh Lane, which was later renamed Prussia Street. In 1749, with a view to further expanding his business, he leased from his brother-in-law Philip Crampton (married to Mary Rathborne) a new dwelling-house on the 'south side of Essex Street with the warehouse behind it, bounded on the west by a passage from Essex Street to Crampton Court', for a period of 147 years. The property was at number 44, right next door to the Dolphin Hotel, a 'popular tavern and coffee-house'. (During the 1840s, in John Rathborne's time, it was Mary Smith who called 'time' at the Dolphin Hotel and the valuation on the tavern was sixty shillings per annum; in 1852 it was managed by a James Flanagan; it still functioned as an inn during the 1970s, when its Bierkeller was a popular haunt of the young set of the day. It now houses the offices of the Family Law and Civil divisions of the Dublin Metropolitan District Court.)

With all aspects of the Rathborne candle-manufacturing business now firmly under the control of William, Joseph junior leased part of his own inherited property at Boot Lane to a Thomas Faielough in 1750, and around the same time took possession of 'a storehouse and yard on Pill-lane'. This he developed into a candle-manufacturing and storage operation. Later that same year his brother-in-law John Marsden, also a candle-maker, took a lease on the remainder of the premises at Boot Lane, together with 'the Chandler's Workhouse and other improvements then standing thereon for a term of fifty-one years from Joseph Rathborne'. It is worth noting that, according to a letter written by Joseph Rathborne, John Marsden's wife Alice Rathborne took a 'deep interest in her husband John's affairs and especially in the manufactury'.

Candle Dips

Around this time the cheapest tallow candles were called dips, after the method of manufacture. The chandler prepared dipped candles by arranging a number of wicks on rods – called broaches – which were about three feet long. Holding the broach on each end he then lowered the wicks into a rectangular vessel filled with molten tallow; the wicks were quickly raised, coated with a thin layer of tallow. They were then hung on a rack until the tallow had sufficiently hardened to retain a new coat on fresh immersion. This operation was repeated until the candles had reached the required thickness. Finally the peaked ends were removed by passing them over a heated brass plate.

According to a description in 1749, the chandler would dip up to three broaches simultaneously but it was nonetheless a slow and laborious business. However, the invention of the dipping frame in the late 1700s greatly increased the number of candles that could be dipped at a time. Superior to the dip candle was the mould candle, generally thought to have originated in France in the fifteenth century but not in use in Ireland until the late 1600s. There were three principal sizes, eights (of which eight candles made a pound in weight), tens and twelves. The cost of candles around this time was eight shillings for a dozen packets of candles of ten-to-the-pound weight. In the mid-1800s the cheapest dips sold for sixpence

A tallow chandler dipping wicks on a broach into a trough of liquid fat. From the 'Universal Magazine of Knowledge and Pleasure', 1749.

a pound while wax candles, always expensive, sold for two shillings per pound.

Using both his finances – which may have been swelled by his marriage to a wealthy jeweller's daughter – and his many business contacts, William built up his business, securing contracts to light the streets of Dublin city and supplying businesses both in Ireland and in Britain. Though by the mid-1700s candle-making had changed very little from the methods that had been in use over the previous centuries, William improved the packaging and presentation of his product in order to increase sales. Under his father's will of 1738 he was left some property on the north side of St Mary's Lane and this he immediately assigned to his brother, the Reverend Richard Rathborne, for the sum of one hundred pounds. Richard had no contact with the family business, preferring to burn candles in his church rather than make them.

William then decided to acquire some lands well outside the city boundaries of the time and in 1742 leased from the Right Honourable William Conolly, Dublin, a part of the lands of Dunsink in the parish of Castleknock totalling sixteen acres, two roods and twenty perches. It is possible that William was a man of great vision, for around this time, in the mid-1700s, the city began to expand towards the east and west. Much of this new development, both north and south of the Liffey, was devoted to housing for the upper classes while the poor remained behind in slum conditions in the old city, including Pill Lane and Boot Lane, where the Rathbornes lived and worked. William was acquiring what we today call a greenfield site.

John Rocque, a Huguenot noted for his maps, calculated in his map of 1756 that the city then consisted of 12,060 dwelling-houses, each one with an average of eight persons, giving a total population of 96,480, a figure which is nowadays thought to be an underestimate. He described the citizens as being 'obliging, gentle and courteous'. Among the most notable features on Rocque's map are Nathaniel Clement's residence in the Phoenix Park (the present-day Áras an Uachtaráin), Drumcondra Lane and Clontarf Island. The map includes all the areas where Rathborne's was active at this

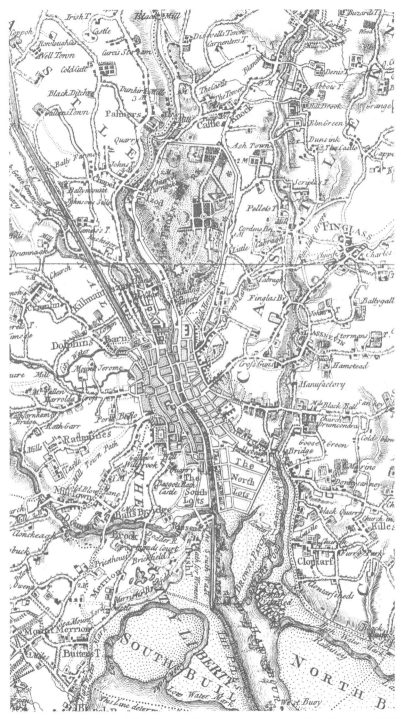

A map of the County of Dublin, divided into Baronies, by John Rocque, 1762

time, including Essex-street, Pill-lane and St Mary's Abbey, and the
family's parish church of St Michan's in Church Street.

An indication of William's wealth around this time can be gleaned
from the fact that his daughter Anne, who married Mongo
Campbell in 1760, had her wedding announcement appear in the
Dublin Gazette as follows: 'Married a few days ago, Mongo
Campbell Esq, Captain in the 55th Regiment of Foot, to Miss
Rathborne, daughter of Mr. William Rathborne, an eminent Wax
Chandler in Essex Street. A young lady possessed of beauty, merit
and a considerable fortune.' Following the death of Mongo
Campbell, Anne married a Colonel Price.

A Country Practice

In 1763 William renewed his lease of Dunsink and it was about this
time that he erected a house and a candle factory and storehouse on
part of the lands he had acquired close to Dunsink and called
Scribblestown (or Scripplestown). The fine stone house was built
from materials extracted from a nearby quarry. Here he
concentrated the output of the business, using the Essex Street
premises for stores and offices. Thus were sown the seeds for the
Ashtown factory and home at Dunsinea and Scribblestown that
were to remain in the Rathborne name for over one hundred and
fifty years. Castleknock and its environs, including Abbottstown,
Ashtown, Dunsink and Scribblestown, was once the domain of the
powerful Anglo-Norman Tyrrell dynasty, Barons of Castleknock.
Strongbow had granted the district to his ally Hugh Tyrrell, and
on the site near the present-day Castleknock College stood
Castleknock Castle. In the early part of the sixteenth century a later
Hugh Tyrrell, the last of the Barons of Castleknock, lived there.
The countryside around Castleknock, including Dunsinea, was
deeply wooded, covered by the dense forest called Scald Wood,
which then stretched from Cabra out as far as the village of
Blanchardstown. Records show that as late as 20 December 1652
the government ordered a hunt of wolves at Castleknock. So it was
in this historic area that William Rathborne established his
chandlery in 1764. In his *History of County Dublin*, published during

the 1800s, the noted historian Francis Erlington Ball records the Rathborne inhabitation of the district in the late 1700s as follows:

> Towards the end of that century a place called Elm Green was the residence of Richard Malone who was interested in pictures and prints and Scribblestown became the home of the Rathborne family. During that time Dunsink was also selected, on account of its commanding position and proximity to Dublin, as the site of the Observatory, founded by the University of Dublin.

When William took time off from his busy routine it is possible that he viewed or took part in the Procession of the Guilds, and from Gilbert's *Calendar of Dublin Records* it is possible to recall the account of the procession of 1767, when William was at the height of his business success. Each guild proceeded in the order drawn for the Procession; the guild of tallow chandlers was twelfth in line, dressed in two shades of blue. An extract from *The Poem of the Procession* describes, in the most colourful of terms, the progress of the guild as it marched through the streets of Dublin:

> Next march the Tallow-chandlers, who expel
> With cheerful lights, shades from the darkest cell
> Enthusiasts of inward light may boast
> But these are they, illuminate the most.

There was a happy day for William in June 1774 when his eldest son, Joseph, married Anne, daughter of Robert Madden of Meadesbrook, Co. Meath. Joseph was not enamoured of the candle-manufacturing business and chose a career in the legal profession. Five years later, in 1779, with the business prospering considerably, William Rathborne died and the business and land came into the possession of his second son, also called William. The young William took firm control of the enterprise, managing to retain the lucrative contract for the lighting of the city of Dublin. He constructed a new storehouse at Dunsinea and bought some adjoining fields. He built stables, purchased horses and established his own fleet of carters to take his products to their market destinations. Life was not all business for the young chandler and on

Original storehouse at Dunsinea, built by William c.1890, now disused and boarded up

(PHOTO BERNARD NEARY)

8 November 1784 he married, by Prerogative Licence, Florence Elizabeth Anne, eldest daughter of William Irvine, MP and Justice of the Peace, of Castle Irvine in County Fermanagh. The marriage ceremony took place in St Brigid's Church, Castleknock, and was performed by the Reverend James Hastings. Part of the marriage settlement made by William on his bride included 'two fields, being part of the lands of Scribblestown (six acres, two perches), part of Dunsink (sixteen acres), in the Parish of Castleknock, part of Bodeen (four acres), a plot of ground on the south side of Essex Street and also £6000 to hold in trust for the issue of the marriage.' The settlement shows how prosperous the Rathborne candle-making business had become. William and Florence had three children, St George, William and Henry.

Business was indeed good, and in a continuing expansion of his trade in 1782, William leased a piece of land in Essex Street, 'a parcel of ground on the east side of the passage from Essex Street to Crampton Court bounded by the holding belonging to William Rathborne and on the west by the passage', and constructed a storehouse on the site. In that same year he leased a house on the south side of Essex Street 'lately known as the King's Arms to hold for forty-four years'. These properties were probably acquired to facilitate the expansion of his stores and offices and not as gifts to pass on to his children in the future. William had built up the business by expanding the factory and adding new stores in the Dunsinea complex, and was no doubt very pleased when his sons Henry and William entered the trade. His third son, St George, took no interest or involvement in the business; he married Martha Mary Knipe and in 1818 was living in Raheny, which was then a scenic rural location in County Dublin. There are no records to show what he did in life, but as Martha Knipe remarried in 1830 (to Marcus Gale), he must have died sometime prior to that.

A major factor in facilitating the expansion and development of the Rathborne works at Ashtown was the construction of the Royal Canal in 1790, which would have provided a convenient mode of transport for its products to the city and to major inland locations along the route of the canal. It appears also that around this time production was consolidated, with the Essex Street premises being used solely for offices, stores and dispatch functions and all candle manufacturing taking place in the rural peace of Dunsinea, supply-ing country and export markets, including a special order for the British House of Lords.

Though work and family life preoccupied him, William devoted much of his spare time to his local parish of St Brigid's in Castleknock. The business was now running very well and employed local labour drawn from Blackhorse-lane (now Avenue) nearby and from the small villages of Ashtown and Blanchardstown. The contract for supplying Dublin with its public street lighting – then solely candle-powered – and contracts for supplying public buildings like Green Street Courthouse with candlelight kept the firm in constant production. William maintained these contracts and for more than thirty prosperous years he was at the helm of the family enterprise. By the time of his death in 1810 the workshops at Dunsinea had grown and expanded considerably.

Following family tradition the business passed into the hands of

Dunsinea Manor, built c.1760

(PHOTO BERNARD NEARY)

William's young son Henry, born in 1790 and a great-grandson of Joseph Rathborne whose will has been mentioned previously. Henry immersed himself in the affairs of the company and in 1811 he leased some more land at Scribblestown and Ashtown and built himself a fine house, calling it 'Dunsinea'; this house is now incorporated within the Teagasc complex of the National Food Centre, the old Agricultural Institute. It has been well preserved and is a fine testament to the architecture of the period. He married Jane, the second daughter of the Reverend Henry Bayly or Baily, of Bayly Farm, Nenagh, County Tipperary, and their children included William Prittie, Henry Bayly, who took his BL degree at Trinity College, John Garnett, who was destined to bring the company into its golden years from the 1830s through to the late 1880s, Jane, born in December 1815, Isabella, and Kate Florence Prittie, born in September 1819.

Henry had obviously decided to establish roots in Dunsinea and he purchased a burial plot in the grounds of his parish church of St Brigid's, nestled in the rural village of Castleknock, a few miles away. There he erected a family vault, with the inscription '*Je ne*

Change Quen Mourant', the motto of the Rathborne family of Scribblestown (Dunsinea) and Kilcogy. Members of his brother William's family lived beside him, but Henry ran the candle factory on his own. It was around this time that the pattern of developing the farm in order to provide work for the staff during off-peak periods commenced. It is also around this time that a factory manager was given a residence within the factory complex, thus freeing the head of the Rathborne household to pursue other business and farming interests.

Through Henry's association with Jane Bayly, William became acquainted with her sister Penelope Mary, and they eventually married and moved into the old family home beside the factory, built in the 1760s by his grandfather, also called William – it is presently the home of Aidan Prior and called 'Dunsinea Manor'. William and Penelope Rathborne had a large family, which included William Humphrey, born on 16 July 1819, who in his middle and late teens took a very keen interest in the candle manufacturing which was very capably run by his cousin John; Robert St George, Georges Lowther, Jane Florence, Penelope, Isabella Sophia, Emily Adelaide and Helen. William, who was himself a JP and a High Sheriff for County Dublin in 1811, later established roots in Kilcogy, County Cavan, where the Rathborne family were already represented. In 1834 he became High Sheriff for that county.

Members of this Kilcogy seat of the Rathborne family later emigrated in the 1880s. Joseph Rathborne, son of Henry Talbot Rathborne and Catherine Caffrey, left Virginia, Co. Cavan, for Chicago, where he met and married Katherine Louise van Schaack. (Joseph's brother William Walter also emigrated to Chicago, in 1889.) Following the birth of his only son, Joseph Cornelius, on 13 September 1883, he moved to Louisiana, where he established the Rathborne Land and Lumber Company. He died in August 1923. His grandson, also called Joseph Cornelius, born on 17 June 1909, served in the Second World War as a major in the US Army. He was aide-de-camp to the commander-in-chief of the 8th Air Force. The lumber company was still in family hands in the 1960s, one Joseph Cornelius, the great-grandson of Joseph, being cited as chairman

Remains of coal-fired boiler house, Dunsinea

(PHOTO BERNARD NEARY)

and chief executive of the firm. An interesting insert in the 1998 accommodation guide for New Orleans shows a Rathbone Inn, located on Esplanade Avenue.

A third sister of Jane Bayly, Helen, married William Rowan Hamilton, the famous mathematician, who discovered the fundamental formula for quaternion multiplication in a flash of genius while walking with Helen along the Royal Canal at Broome Bridge, Cabra West. He carved out the formula on the stone of the bridge with a rock: "$I^2 = J^2 = K^2 = ijk = -1$". A plaque on the bridge, erected in 1954, commemorates the discovery. Rowan Hamilton was the Director of Dunsink Observatory, which had an entrance beside that of Dunsinea, at the top of the roadway leading into the factory and residential complex. He developed a close friendship with his near-neighbours Henry and William Rathborne and through them became acquainted with their sister-in-law Helen.

Rowan Hamilton became 'Uncle Hamilton' to the family of Henry and Jane Rathborne to distinguish him from the other uncle with the same Christian name, William Rathborne. An extract from a notebook of Henry's daughter Kate Florence Prittie gives an account of the mathematical exercises set for her by her famous uncle. The mathematician doted on his sister-in-law's daughter; Grave's *Life of Rowan Hamilton* states that Kate 'became to her uncle a favourite relative'. It is interesting to note that there still exists an old right-of-way between Dunsinea and Dunsink, which must have been established by the comings and goings between the Rathborne households and that of Rowan Hamilton at the Observatory. Rowan Hamilton was a member of the Church of Ireland and the three couples, with their families, would have made the beautiful carriage journey together every Sunday to St Brigid's church in Castleknock village.

Mining Industry

Rathborne's was a major supplier of candles and oil to the Irish mining industry, which existed in numerous locations around the country, prospering in the 1800s. Major mining companies operated at Allihies, Avoca (where five companies operated mines), Knockmahon, Lackamore, Cosheen and Kenmare. The mining industry provided an important outlet for Rathborne's, and old company records show that they supplied candles to the Avoca and Knockmahon mines in Leinster. Avoca was a busy mining centre in the early-to-mid 1800s, and around 1840 it was reported that a thousand carters were subcontracted to bring the ore to Arklow or Wicklow. Between 1835 and 1844 approximately 77,000 tons of copper and 232,000 tons of pyrite were mined at Avoca, to a value of £750,000. The mine employed two thousand people directly. As a result it was a lucrative contract for the candle-supplier. Candles were purchased directly from Rathborne's by the mine owners, and the miners then purchased the candles from their employers for use in the mine shafts. Oral historical sources suggest that employers sold the candles that they purchased in bulk from Rathborne's to their underground miners at a profit.

The use of candlelight in mines at this time was described thus by a visitor to the Allihies mine in west Cork: 'Onward and onward through passage after passage went the miners, illuminated only by the wretched dips which swiltered over their candlesticks, gluing fingers together and spluttering or extinguishing as the case may be according to the size or aim of the drip from above.' The same visitor described the work in the mines, which was carried out 'in the flickering light of foul-smelling tallow candles. And as long as the candles flickered there was enough oxygen.' When they gutted, new air pipes had to be led to the workface or new internal vent shafts opened.

Besides providing a valuable source of light, and being an indication of the quality of air deep below the earth's surface, the tallow candles could also be used as a source of food if a miner was trapped underground for a period of time. With improvements in technology miners' helmets were introduced with a candle-lamp fitted. In the mid-1800s the candle-lamp was replaced in the mines by the oil lamp and later still by battery light. Miners continued, however, to use candles to indicate the level of oxygen in the mine. The candle was also used as a measure of miners' shifts up to the middle of the present century. Indeed, as late as 1949 Rathborne's was producing a special type of candle used in the coal mines of County Kilkenny solely for this purpose.

Lighthouses

In this day and age it is hard to believe that at one time lighthouses were illuminated by the humble candle. Before the candle it was burning coal that showed the light – the last open coal fire to be in use as a light source in a British lighthouse was at St Bees, on the Cumbrian coast, in 1823. Candles undoubtedly functioned as light sources in medieval lighthouses but no details have survived. By the sixteenth century candles were being used to provide leading lights which shone only in a narrow sector and guided mariners along a safe route, often into a harbour. A single tallow candle was the source in a leading light built at North Shields, on the Tyne and Wear in the north-east of England, in 1540. The famous Eddystone Lighthouse was still lit by candles until it was taken over by Trinity House in 1807.

In Ireland the provision of coastal lights was the responsibility of a number of bodies, beginning with the Commissioners for Barracks in 1767; in 1796 the Customs Board took over and then in

1810 responsibility passed on to the Corporation for Preserving and Improving the Port of Dublin, and the lighthouse department of this body was commonly known as the Ballast Office. Finally, by an Act of Parliament in 1867, two new public boards were established to perform the functions previously carried out by the Corporation for Preserving and Improving the Port of Dublin, namely the Dublin Port and Docks Board to look after port functions and the Commissioners of Irish Lights to take over the responsibility of maintaining the system of lighthouses around the coast.

There were also a number of lighthouses in the control of individuals, as private lighthouse ownership was a profitable enterprise and enjoyed great popularity with investors during the late seventeenth century. In Ireland, Sir Robert Reading built five lighthouses along the east and south-eastern coasts in the 1660s. Rathborne's supplied many of the caretakers or owners of the privately run lighthouses directly and as a result records are very poor. Henry Rathborne supplied candles for the bright little lighthouse at Balbriggan harbour, perched precariously on the end of the six-hundred-foot pier. An extant record shows 'one William Rathborne' supplying '200 dozen candles of good manufacture' to the lighthouse in 1805 – the year of the Battle of Trafalgar. The lighthouse, with its eight-foot-diameter lantern, was built in 1769, and the Hamilton family, from Hampton Hall, who had supervised the building of the harbour from 1761 to 1765, were also responsible for the erection and maintenance of the lighthouse. It is worth noting that the Rathbornes were next-door neighbours to some members of the Hamilton family, who resided at Abbottstown House and who are also buried in the churchyard at St Brigid's, Castleknock. The glass lantern was frequently broken by high seas and in 1820, as a result of recommendations by the Reverend George Hamilton, the tower was increased in height by the Ballast Board and the source of light was altered from candle power to 'five oil lamps and each with a reflector.' The first supply of oil, a 'high quality spermaceti oil', was supplied by 'Mr. Henry Rathborne esquire, Dunsinea, Cabragh'. It is interesting to note that this lighthouse was downgraded to a minor harbour light in 1860 and was not converted to electricity until 3 October 1960.

Candlelight at Wicklow

The candle was a surprisingly effective light source, particularly when used with a reflector. A candle provided the harbour light at Bridport, in Dorset, England, as late as 1861. Candelabra were used where a stronger source of light was required; the light at the UK's first Eddystone, Winstanley's tower of 1698, was a candelabrum of at least twenty-six candles. By 1810 only one location under the control of the Ballast Board was illuminated by candlelight – at Wicklow, where two lighthouses were supplied by Henry Rathborne.

The two lighthouses used a considerable quantity of candles. George Darby, contractor for maintaining both Wicklow light-houses, wrote to the Ballast Office in 1811 stating that 'the consumption of candles at the station for the six months 24 December 1810 to 24 June 1811 was 370 dozen, at a Contract rate of 6/= per dozen candles'. However, he went on to state that due to the prevailing market prices he had to pay twelve shillings per dozen for one hundred dozen and eleven shillings per dozen for three hundred dozen (thirty dozen of the four hundred dozen candles purchased were not used during the period). He then petitioned the Ballast Board for the balance of one hundred and five pounds. Leonard Manly, Head Keeper at Wicklow Lighthouse, 'made oath on the Holy Evangelists before William Coates JP, of Wicklow Town' that the account in question 'was a true statement of accounts'. The Board paid the one hundred and five pounds and according to old Rathborne records, these candles were supplied by Henry Rathborne. Leonard Manly, like all the lighthouse-keepers at the time, was allowed to keep the butts of the used candles as a bonus – quite a perk in the days when candles were the only source of domestic light. The butts of the perfectly edible tallow candles also provided an important supplement to their diet on occasions when food rations were running low.

Tenders Sought

When the lighthouse authorities were looking for supplies of raw materials they sought competitive tenders. The following is a copy of a newspaper tender notice dated 7 March 1834:

> The Corporation for Preserving and Improving the Port of Dublin will receive proposals for the supply of 95 tuns* of the best Spermaceti Oil for the lighthouses on the coast of Ireland. The oil to be delivered at the Ballast Office Store, North Wall, Dublin. 40 tuns on or before the 17th day of April next and the remainder, 55 tuns, on or before the 17th day of May next, in strong well-hooped casks not containing more than 55 gallons each. Tenders to be sealed and endorsed "Tenders for the Supply of Oil for Lighthouses on the Coast of Ireland" to be sent to the Secretary, John Cossart Esq. on or before 25th March 1834. Samples of the oil to be sent with the proposals. Security will be required for the due performance of the Contract. – Ballast Office, Dublin, 7th March 1834.

Henry Rathborne's bid of '£69.6.0d per tun of two-hundred and fifty-two gallons' was successful to secure this particular contract. The securities were given by Robert Johnson of number 7 Mountjoy Square East and William Reiley of Westmoreland Street, Dublin. Rathborne's was initially the major candle supplier and later the dominant spermaceti and paraffin oil supplier to lighthouses around the country. The records of the Ballast Board show an entry for 27 April 1820: 'To Henry Rathborne, the sum of £748=1=3d for the supply of high-quality spermaceti oil.' The contract to supply first the Ballast Board and then the Commissioners of Irish Lights from 1810 onwards was quite a valuable one for Henry and John Rathborne. In 1820 Henry became a major supplier of spermaceti; a sample of his business with the Ballast Board over a ten-year period is reproduced herein as Appendix V. John Garnett Rathborne continued supplying the lighthouse service when he succeeded his

---

* A tun is a measure of liquid capacity, especially wine, and is the equivalent of 252 gallons.

father Henry in 1836. The lighthouse business was indeed a lucrative one, as can be gleaned from the following prices taken from the Board's records:

1 June 1820:

    20 tuns of Spermaceti oil from H Rathborne at 6/8d per late Irish gallon;

11 Apr 1822:

    20 tuns of Spermaceti oil from H Rathborne at 5/= per late Irish gallon;

6 Mar 1823:

    60 tuns of Spermaceti oil from H Rathborne at 3/10d per late Irish gal.;

31 Mar 1825:

    75 tuns of Spermaceti oil from H Rathborne at 4/3d per late Irish gal.;

21 Dec 1826:

    70 tuns of Spermaceti oil from H Rathborne at 5/4d per imperial gallon;

24 Jan 1828:

    70 tuns of Spermaceti oil from H Rathborne at 6/6d per imperial gallon;

19 Feb 1829:

    75 tuns of Spermaceti oil from H Rathborne at 6/9d per imperial gallon.

Illuminants

By the early 1820s Ireland's lighthouses were illuminated by oil, the standard lamp was the Argand lamp and the common fuel in use was 'best quality spermaceti oil' extracted from the head of the sperm whale. The Argand lamp, introduced in Europe in 1784, was designed by the Swiss inventor Ami Argand. It had a hollow, circular wick that permitted oxygen to travel up the inside and outside surfaces, giving a brighter light equivalent to that of seven candles. The reflectors were made from thin copper sheets that were moulded into a parabolic shape and silvered on the inside to maximise the light reflection. The reflectors were mounted behind the lamp to concentrate all light from the flame in an outward direction. The number of lamps and reflectors employed determined the intensity of the light, which in turn defined the purpose of the lighthouse, for example a landfall light or a harbour light. Argand lamps and parabolic reflectors are still in use and currently employed at lighthouse stations around the country; for example, there are twenty-nine at Poolbeg Lighthouse and twenty-seven at Cape Clear Island and Old Head of Kinsale.

The consumption of spermaceti oil per Argand lamp was in the region of twenty gallons a year. During the period 1840–50 the price of spermaceti rose so much that it was replaced by colza oil, derived from rape seed. Other oils used included herring oil and seal oil, and Rathborne's also supplied these particular fuels to the lighthouse service. Around 1870 mineral oil (kerosene) became the common lighthouse fuel; also around this time coal gas was produced and used at some lighthouses. Towards the end of the 1800s the incandescent vapour lamp, burning paraffin oil, was employed at most lighthouses around the coast. This lamp and its ancillary equipment pressurised paraffin oil to cause it to vaporise and in this state it was burned in a mantle, similar to a gas light. The light emitted was a very bright, clean light which was well suited to the Fresnel lens in use in most lighthouses at that time. Ever competitive, Rathborne's succeeded in securing the bulk of the Commissioners' orders for the supply of paraffin oil.

Incandescent light was in general use in Irish lighthouses right up to the 1960s and 1970s, when electricity finally became the major illuminant. Electricity first came on the Irish lighthouse scene when it was introduced at Donaghadee in 1936. Most offshore lighthouse stations generate their own electricity while land-based stations are connected into the national grid. A small number of minor stations still use gas as an illuminant. It is amazing to note that from the 1700s to the present day John G. Rathborne & Company has, under its own name or latterly that of its parent, Irish Shell Limited, been a supplier of raw materials to the Irish Lighthouse Service. At some periods during this time they were the sole supplier while at other periods they fulfilled a secondary supply role. It is certainly a remarkable track record in supplier–customer relations in the ever-changing world of business.

Street Lighting

During the 1700s and 1800s street lighting in Dublin was provided by the candle, and Rathborne's was one of the more successful of those chandlers that secured the tender for the lighting of the city. The days of street candle lighting ended in the early 1800s. In the *Dublin Assembly Roll* for 1805 it is recorded that the Corporation expressed concern at the fact that 'the streets were encumbered with filth and the pavement continues in universal ruin'. There is no mention of dissatisfaction with the lighting of the city. However, as a result of that concern the Corporation set up a committee, which included Arthur Guinness (of the famous brewing family), 'to report on the paving, lighting, cleansing etc. of Dublin'. This step was later to lead to the introduction of gas lighting and the end of the era of public candle lighting. The candle-manufacturing industry did put up a spirited fight to protect this lucrative market and they had a powerful voice on the Corporation, which petitioned Henry Grattan, MP, to have the Gas Light Bill set aside. Such lobbying by the industry was initially successful, as is obvious from the following letter, dated 8 May 1817 and posted from 29 Duke Street, London:

> To the honourable the Sheriffs of Dublin, Messieurs Dixon and Read. Sirs – I mentioned in my former letter to you, that I had presented your Petition against the Gas Light Bill, according to your wishes. I have now the satisfaction to tell you, that Mr. Peel from his great respect for the wishes of the city has given up the Bill. I have the honour to be your most faithful and obedient servant, Henry Grattan.

Henry Rathborne received the good news from Grattan in a letter dated 9 May 1817. However, the matter of the installation of street gas lighting did not go away and its introduction was again in the public arena the following year. The Lord Lieutenant, in mooting a new gaslight bill in 1818, was petitioned by Henry Rathborne in December of that year with regard to 'the public safety, which must be affected by the manufacture and conduction of gas'. The following year the Corporation requested the Lord

Lieutenant to furnish it with a copy of the intended Gas Light Bill in order that it 'may consider the propriety of a measure that must lay a very heavy additional expense on the citizens'. On 7 June 1820 the committee set up by the Corporation to enquire into and report upon the Gas Light Bill found that:

> From the specimens we have had of Gas, as manufactured in the city by the agents and promoters of the measure, and from the noxious vapour and deleterious effects produced by it, the health and comfort of the inhabitants have been materially injured, and the water in several streets through which it is conducted has been rendered totally unfit for use. We therefore highly disapprove of lighting the city of Dublin with Gas.

Henry Rathborne led a number of delegations to petition the Lord Mayor and Aldermen of Dublin, a heavy duty at the time for a young man of around twenty-seven years of age. The reluctance of the Corporation to embrace gas lighting, which would be more efficient and effective than candlelight, was probably due to the heavy cost involved; but in the end the efforts of Henry and the candle industry, and the caution of the Corporation, did not stop the march of progress and the Act of Lighting the City and Suburbs of Dublin with Gas (I George IV) came into force in 1821. It turned out that the worst fears of the Corporation with regard to the 'deleterious effects' of gas did not come true and in the summer of 1824 the Mansion House itself, the home of the Lord Mayor, was fitted out for gas light 'at a cost of £210=17s=2d, after giving credit for £25=0s=0d for old materials'. Difficult trading conditions for Rathborne's followed the loss of the lucrative contract to provide Dublin city with its street-lighting, but under the capable guidance of Henry, the company survived in the business and continued to enjoy prosperity in its ancient craft of candle-making.

Repeal of Candle Tax

Henry was probably delighted to see the repeal of the Candle Tax in 1831, which resulted in a more favourable business climate for the trade. However, his delight did not last very long as a terrible personal tragedy struck him on New Year's Day in 1833 with the sudden death of his nineteen-year-old son William Prittie Rathborne. Henry was deeply affected by the death. A vibrant, enterprising and youthful head of the chandlery, Henry Rathborne took ill and died suddenly on 1 July 1836, at just forty-six years of age. His wife Jane outlived him by thirteen years. She died, at the age of sixty-two, in July 1849 and was buried beside her husband in the family vault in St Brigid's churchyard on 8 August 1849.

The cash element of Henry's will, which was proved in 1837, amounted to £21,000 – a very considerable sum in those days. The business of wax-chandlering was left to the family under similar terms as those incorporated in the will of Joseph, the great-grandfather, and the chandlery then passed into the hands of Henry's son John Garnett Rathborne – The John G. in the present-day company name – who was born in 1820 and was only seventeen years old when he took charge of the business. Of course, his brother Henry B. and his uncle William were there to lend a hand, living adjacent to the factory premises. In any event John had been groomed to succeed his father – the records of the Commissioners of Irish Lights show that some actual payments were requested by and made to him during 1835, the year before Henry's death. After July 1836 all the Commissioner's accounts with the firm appear in the name of John Rathborne.

On 25 June 1840 Henry's eldest daughter, Jane Bentley, married the Reverend Thomas Luby, a Fellow of Trinity College. A letter which survived in the company's files throws some interesting light on the family. The letter is marked 'private' with the initials JR on the front of the envelope – John Rathborne, brother of Jane – and is signed John. Hand-written, it reads as follows:

> The Rev Thos Luby DD, FTCD. Dear Tom, I write to acknowledge the receipt of your draft this day for £250 for which as well as for a former draft to the same amount, I am now your debtor. This sum of five hundred pounds I promise to repay you at any time on your giving me three months notice, and to pay, whilst I hold it, in my hands,

months notice, and to pay, whilst I hold it, in my hands, interest at the rate of 5% per annum. Yours etc. John.

Isabella, the apple in Henry's eye, was under-age when she married Walter Keating, a widower and barrister of Sylvan Park, Kells, County Meath, on 4 November 1845. It is possible that Isabella got to know Walter through her father, for her new husband's father – also called Walter – was, like Henry, a magistrate. The marriage took place in St Brigid's, and the ceremony was conducted by Reverend Franc Sadlier, Reverend Ralph Sadlier being ill at the time. The witnesses were Jane Bentley and her husband Thomas Luby. The same month Penelope, the wife of William Rathborne, was buried in the family vault in St Brigid's; she was just fifty-two years old and died on 22 November 1845.

Lively Trade

Even though oil lamps, and later gas lighting, affected the market for Rathborne's candles, there was still a huge demand for them throughout the 1800s, as can be seen from this extract from William Makepeace Thackeray's *Irish Sketch-Book*, where the author tells of how he had been wined and dined in Dublin:

> At Mr. Lovegrowe's the main course was lobster, which was shelled, coated with a mixture of mustard, vinegar, catsup and strong cayenne pepper, and cooked in an affair called a dispatcher, over whisky; a glass-and-a-half of sherry was added to the pan; the lobster was served hot and eaten on the spot under *wax candle-light*. Porter is commonly drunk with this and whisky punch afterwards and the dish is fit for an emperor.

Later, at Kildare Street, there was 'white neck-cloths, black waiters, *wax-candles* and some of the best wine in Europe', and at a publisher's home he had '*wax-candles* and some of the best wine in Europe', at Mr. Lever's, '*wax-candles* and some of the best wine in Europe'. From reading Thackeray (1811–63) one gets an idea of the importance of the candle as a source of power in the days preceding mains gas-light and electrification, and also the social status of the wax candle over the common tallow candle, which was the light source of the masses.

In 1839 young William Humphry Rathborne married Elizabeth, daughter of Col. Hans Allen of the Royal Artillery, and their children included Hans Robert, St George John, Henry Humphry and William Hans, who was born on 21 December 1841 and who married Bella Grace, daughter of John D. McNeale, of Charlcote, Cheltenham, on 3 July 1879. Ten years after that another son, St George John, married Bella's sister Margaret in the British Embassy in Paris, on 22 April 1889. St George was by this time a British Army major serving in the 66th Regiment. Descendants of both of these marriages were living in the Cheltenham district in the 1960s.

During the 1840s an Edward Wade was employed by John G. Rathborne at Dunsinea and the only surviving wages account from this period is a receipt for wages paid to him in 1844. It reads:

> Received from Messrs J. & H. Rathborne the sum of twelve pounds ten shillings sterling, being amount of my quarter salary due and ended 3rd day of January 1844. £12.10s.0d. Dated this 3rd day of January 1844 (Signed) Edward Wade.

Despite his commitments to the trade and his duties as a Justice of the Peace, John still had some time for pleasure. On 7 September 1846 he shared an eclipse of the sun with his entire work force, from the vantage point of the hill to the rear of the factory storehouse. According to the records of Dunsink Observatory, 'the eclipse was visible at Dunsinea and commenced at 11.45am and finished at 2.38pm'. There was a happy occasion for John on 29 November 1848 when his first cousin Robert St George Rathborne (born 3 October 1821), son of William, of Scribblestown House, married Grace Coffey, who hailed from Newcastle, Co. Westmeath. The ceremony was carried out by the Reverend George Stone, and Jane Bentley was one of the witnesses. They settled in Cabra and it is interesting to note that a confessional box in St Peter's Roman Catholic Church, Phibsborough, was erected by them in memory of one of their daughters. Robert took no interest in the candle trade, however, using candles only to study his law books during the hours of darkness, and he became a barrister. Another first cousin, Penelope, a sister of Robert St George, married Grace Coffey's brother Richard.

The famine years of the late 1840s were difficult trading years for the candle factory, but the tenacity of John G. and his strong business acumen helped it through. The Rathborne family were not unaffected by the horrors sweeping the country during the famine years. John G.'s cousin Isabella Sophia, who was born on 5 December 1826 and who married a Major Longworth on 10 January 1849, died in May of that same year, aged twenty-three. Tragically, her younger sister Emily Adelaide died suddenly the next day, 21 May 1849, aged just nineteen years. It is reasonable to assume that the deaths of these two young women were a result of pestilence associated with the Famine. Both sisters were buried in St Peter's Churchyard, Athlone. There is a plaque, erected by a broken-hearted Major Longworth, commemorating the two sisters in St Brigid's Church, Castleknock, which testifies to Isabella's 'kind and endearing manners' and refers to her many virtues, which 'caused her to be loved and esteemed by all who knew her'. The famine affected all communities, rich and poor, and all religious persuasions – in one day alone in 1847 there were seven burials in St Brigid's churchyard.

During the 1850s Rathborne's continued to prosper in business. As the industrial market for candles contracted with the introduction of piped gas, the company increased its activity in a growing domestic market. By the mid-1800s almost all new factories and institutions in Dublin city were connected to a gas supply; for example, when HM Prison, Mountjoy, opened for business on Dublin's North Circular Road in 1850, it was lit by gas, though some areas of the prison had no gas connections and candles supplied the light. As a result the prison always kept large supplies of candles in the storeroom. The night-duty officers carried candle lamps; they used these to inspect the cells, which they placed in a special opening in the door at waist level. They inserted the lamp, which illuminated the cell, and then checked on the prisoner inside through the spy hole. These small sliding openings can still be seen in some of the old cell doors in the prison. The Fenian leader Jeremiah O'Donovan Rossa, whose trial (if it could be called that) commenced in Green Street Courthouse on 29 November 1865 and who was lodged in Mountjoy Prison in December of that year, recalls the use of candlelight in the prison in his book *My Years in English Jails*, first published by the American News Company in New York in 1874:

> Five minutes after the condemnation I was ushered unto the black van; in fact, it had been waiting for me two hours, the horses ready harnessed and the soldiers equipped, to escort me to Mountjoy prison … there a warder escorted me to my cell, and, giving his command to two others, they came, one holding a candle and the other a razor … my eyes fell on the face of the man who was holding the candle, and they began to swim in their sockets. It was the first time I got soft during my imprisonment, but when I saw the tears streaming down the cheeks of this Irish-hearted jailer who was holding the candle, I could not restrain my own from starting.

Rathborne's supplied the prison with candle stocks from time to time. Candles must have burned in the prison up to at least the early 1900s, judging from an item in the *Prison Rule Book*, which came into force on 24 February 1894. Rule 118 stated that 'an officer neglecting to have the lights, lamps, candles etc. properly trimmed and burning at the times appointed' was subject to a fine of one shilling on the first offence, 1/6d on the second offence and two shillings on the third offence – a hefty sum when one considers that the salary of an ordinary prison warder was just under twenty shillings, or one pound, per week.

A prosperous and expanding middle and lower-middle class in Dublin and other urban centres ensured a continuing market for the candle, as many domestic dwellings only had gaslight supplied on the ground floors. Demand was also helped by the fact that the spread of gaslight to rural districts was not as rapid as the later spread of electricity – for example it was not until 1900 that the State Inebriate Reformatory at Ennis, formerly the Co. Clare Prison, was connected to a gas supply. Prior to that it was illuminated solely by candle and oil-lamp, and in June 1898 Rathborne's supplied fifty boxes of candles of six to the pound to the institution, freighted by rail.

John's uncle William decided to settle in the midlands during the early 1850s and left Scribblestown House for the quiet seclusion of Gay Brook, Mullingar, County Westmeath. On his death at the age of seventy years, his remains were brought back to Castleknock and he was buried in the family vault on 28 September 1857. The burial service was performed by Rev. Ralph Sadlier, assisted by Rev J.D. Cook.

Planning for the Future

At the close of 1865, on 2 November, John Rathborne married Eliza, the daughter of William F. Burnley of London. The marriage terms included 'parts of Ashtown and Irishtown, parts of Scribblestown and a plot of ground on the East side of the Royal Canal, all in the Barony of Castleknock'. John was a man of great foresight and in 1866, with a keen eye to the future, he leased a plot of ground on the North Wall known as 'the Lotts'.

The North Lotts district was, up to the early part of the present century, humorously called Newfoundland on account of its having being reclaimed from the sea, and there is actually a Newfoundland Street within the area's boundary. The district originated following the embankment of the Liffey, which began in 1717 and was completed in 1729 with the erection of the North Wall. The area then bounded by the North Wall, the East Wall, the North Strand and Amiens Street was reclaimed from the sea in the early 1730s. It got its name, the North Lotts, because the Corporation of Dublin in 1717 drew lots for the distribution amongst themselves, the Aldermen and Burgesses of Dublin, of the land now available for acquisition as a result of the construction of the North Wall. They then shared out the reclaimed land in portions called 'lots'. There were dry and wet lots and a map was prepared on which the district was divided into squares, each one containing the name of the fortunate grantee. The dry lots were those which in fact were reclaimed. The wet lots were those which, though marked on the map as granted, still remained covered by tide. However, the proprietorial rights of the grantees of the wet lots remained: in his book *North Dublin City & County*, published in 1909, Dillon Cosgrave states that 'quite recently the Corporation granted compensation to a Dublin gentleman, the direct descendant of the original who owned a wet lot inside the Northern Railway in the space now being reclaimed'.

On the exact spot where Newfoundland Street and Nixon Street are situated Campbell's *Map of Dublin 1811* marks an 'intended floating dock' never actually constructed. The Corporation of Dublin honoured itself in the 'Lotts' by conferring on the new streets laid out there the names Mayor Street, Sheriff Street, Guild Street and Commons Street after the Lord Mayor, the Sheriffs, the Guilds of each trade of which the Corporation was then composed and the Commons who elected them.

The site of Rathborne's present-day factory formed part of the land earmarked by Dublin Corporation for a new, modern cattle market. In the late 1850s it became necessary to relocate the market from Smithfield, which had become overcrowded and inadequate to meet the demands of a growing cattle industry. Housing developments over the years had left no room for growth at Smithfield. The City Engineer, George Hemans, son of the poet Felicia Dorothea Hemans, prepared, in 1860, a blueprint for redevelopment of the market by relocating it in the North Lotts, which had 'facilities for ample pasture' and was an ideal location due to its 'contiguity to the Liffey Branch of the Midland and Great Western Railways (MGWR) and to the packets for shipment to England and elsewhere'. George Hemans was also the engineer responsible for the laying of the MGWR railway line from Dublin to Galway, which passed through the Rathborne property at Castleknock. In December 1861 an application was made to Parliament for leave to introduce a Bill to incorporate a company for the purpose of establishing, erecting and maintaining a new Market, to be called the Metropolitan Cattle Market, for the sale of cattle, horses, sheep, pigs, hides, skins and other marketable commodities; such proposed market being situate in the North Lotts, immediately adjoining the MGWR and extending from the Dublin & Drogheda Railway to the East-road and Sheriff-street, all in the town land of North Lotts, in the parish of St Thomas and county of the city of Dublin. And power will be taken to erect suitable offices, counting-houses, sheds, stores for the sale of provender, dwelling-houses, shops, weighing-machines, water tanks, stalls, pens, slaughterhouses, with all other necessary buildings suitable for the purposes of such proposed Market.

There was concerted and bitter opposition to the relocation of the market to the North Lotts by the trade itself and by July 1862 those opposed to the move had collected, by voluntary subscription, 'an amount of money totalling that which is required for the erection of a suitable market on a desired site adjacent to the Smithfield market'. (For the very interested, a list of the subscribers can be found on page 178 of the *Dublin Builder* dated 15 July 1862.) These efforts paid off, for Dublin Corporation lost interest in its own proposal and on 26 November 1863 the new Dublin Cattle Market was opened on a site at the triangle of land between Aughrim Street, Prussia Street and North Circular Road, which later earned the district the nickname 'Cowtown'.

This simple investment by John at the North Lotts laid the seeds for the eventual transfer and consolidation of the Rathborne business to its present-day location on East Wall Road. At that time the East Wall Road was still called the Wharf Road by the locals, after the slip which was constructed in the 1780s for the use of bathers. The current of the Tolka provided a great depth of water and the slip was in use at the turn of the present century as a bathing area. There was a stone platform at the slip which was used by divers and this was locally referred to as the Smoothing Iron, on account of its shape.

On 10 November 1866, John's only child, Henry Burnley, was born. Henry B. was christened in St Brigid's on 21 December 1866; unknown to his father, the infant was to be the last Rathborne heir to the family business. Less than five months after the christening, John's wife Eliza died, on Sunday 12 May 1867. She was buried in the family vault on 16 May 1867, the Rev. Ralph Sadlier performing the ceremony and providing comfort to John in his time of distress. He was devastated by the death of Eliza – they had been married for less than two years – and in an effort to suppress his grief he devoted ever more time to the chandlery, promoting the firm at more and more exhibitions and expanding the factory at Dunsinea with the construction of a coal-burning pump house and the addition of storage space. At the North Lotts site, which was an extensive one, he built an imposing storehouse and yard, complete with oil storage tanks, in 1868.

At this stage John was a very comfortable businessman and in 1868 was one of three Rathbornes listed in *Thom's Directory*, being mentioned as a Justice of the Peace; his brother Henry Baily Rathborne is listed as a barrister. The third name is that of their cousin Captain William Humphrey Rathborne of Cabra Villa, Phibsborough. Cabra Villa was a large farm covering the present-day area of Cabra West and the farmhouse was situated where Fassaugh Avenue meets Broombridge Road today, adjacent to the roundabout at the Ratoath Road junction. The Captain was a successful farmer and proprietor of the Leinster Dairy. The last resident and owner of Cabra Villa was Christopher Keogh, who vacated it when it was compulsorily purchased by Dublin Corporation and levelled to make way for the most ambitious housing project in Europe in the late 1930s, the suburb of Cabra West.* Christopher's family purchased the property from William H.'s heirs in 1880 and ran a successful dairy business on seven acres

---

* It is interesting to note that Christopher Keogh was also the last resident of Finnstown House in Lucan, now a luxurious hotel and once a Sarsfield family domain.

of land attaching to the farmhouse. Christopher informed the author during an interview in 1983 that he recalled as a child seeing the name H. Rathborne carved out in wood over the door of a big loft at the back of Cabra Villa. The name was still there when he vacated the house before it was demolished by the Corporation. Directly facing Cabra Villa was the huge, imposing mansion of Cabragh House, ancestral family home of the Segrave family and at one stage the country home of John Toler, Lord Norbury, the infamous hanging judge. Old residents of Cabra West say that the ghost of Lord Norbury still haunts the district.

It appears that around 1870 John had streamlined the company's operations by concentrating the firm's office and Dublin city dispatch operations at 44 Essex Street, with candle production and packaging at Dunsinea and rural dispatch operations being gradually introduced to East Wall. The stores at the North Lotts were developed and expanded over the next twenty years so that by 1890 the 'Dublin Petroleum Stores', as it was then called, was where the bulk of Rathborne's candles, oils and raw materials were stored. The work force employed at the extensive storehouses no doubt enjoyed the location, as according to the historian of the day, Dillon Cosgrave, from nearby 'a fine view of Clontarf, Howth and the northern portion of the Bay is obtained'. During the first decade of the present century John's son, Henry Burnley Rathborne, often visited the Dublin Petroleum Stores and during summer months he regularly paused to look at the bathers while on his travels.

As with his predecessors, John was very much involved in church affairs and on 21 June 1870 he was elected to the Select Vestry of St Brigid's; he was re-elected in 1871 and 1872. Around this time Castleknock and environs, including Abbottstown, Scribblestown, Blanchardstown, Ashtown and Dunsinea, from where the Rathbornes drew their labour, had a population of approximately 6000, of which 147 lived in the village of Castleknock, in forty houses. On 28 December 1870, the Feast of the Holy Innocents, as a member of the Select Vestry at St Brigid's, John attended the laying of the foundation stone to St Thomas's Church in Mulhuddart, County Dublin. A year later, on 6 November 1871, he was among those who petitioned Church of Ireland Archbishop Richard Chevenix to consecrate the new church, and the consecration duly took place on 19 December 1871. The little church of St Thomas, which is a simple church with no electricity, to this day serves as a place of worship to the community and is still lit by candlelight. The annual dawn Pentecost service, held at 6.30 a.m., is particularly striking. The present Rector, Canon Paul Colton, purchases all his candles from Rathborne's. John G. Rathborne has been continuously supplying St Thomas's with candles since its construction one hundred and twenty-seven years ago.

Early Vehicle Lighting

In the late 1800s John G. Rathborne was a 'noted supplier of light to the vehicular trade', an area of business that was then growing rapidly. Although horse-drawn carriages were introduced around the middle of the sixteenth century, carriage lamps were not in general use until the mid-1800s because of the risk of violence attaching to night-time travel and the dangerous state of the roads. Around 1850 'evening drives' around the city in horse-drawn carriages became fashionable and candle-powered coach lamps were fitted and in use on most vehicular traffic. However, they were looked upon more as decorative features than as a source of light. Although paraffin as a lighting medium was commercially available from 1854, candle-lamps for carriages remained inexpensive and therefore very popular with traders who at night used hansom cabs, brewers' drays or hand carts. As with domestic consumers of light, the candle was preferred to the competing oil lamp due to its safety and convenience for carrying from room to room or from stable to coach-house. It was therefore sure of its market even if it was not used exclusively. Carriage and self-fitting candles were generally termed *white candles*.

The first challenge to the supremacy of the carriage candle-lamp came in 1892, when an oil-lit device called the *anti-candle* was patented by Salisbury's in the UK. However, functional carriage candle-lamps were still catalogued and available from a number of manufacturers during the 1930s. Kathleen Connolly from Lecklevera, Smithboro, County Monaghan, who was born in 1914, recalls this form of candle illumination:

> My father had two carriage candle-lamps on his pony and trap. The candles, which he bought in the local shop, came from Rathborne's in Dublin and were thick ones with a special end so that, as they burned down, they could be raised up, or screwed upwards, inside the lamp by means of an outside knob. Some evenings when he had to go into Monaghan Town he would light the candles and they would stay lighting for the full journey there and back home. He had to open a little glass door on the lamp-holders to light and blow out the candles, which never went out during a journey. Nothing went to waste – we had six windows in our farmhouse, three upstairs and three downstairs and at Christmas time my father got the butts and placed them in each window, wedged on a piece of slate for a holder. As a little girl I remember when we left the house for midnight Mass in the pony and trap, the six lighted candles looked like little stars as we gazed back at the house. All the butts were used up in this way over Christmas.

With the introduction of the bicycle in the late 1880s and its immediate popularity with the mass public, yet another market appeared for Rathborne's to tap into, and this the firm cleverly did, directing its publicity efforts at the 'Captains of Bicycle Clubs'. However, candle-powered lighting never proved popular with the cycling public although it did enjoy great success with lady cyclists, because of its cleanliness, around the turn of the century and again during the 1930s. Despite Rathborne's advertising claims of 'power and reliability', the bicycle candle-lamp emitted very little light and was almost impossible to keep alight in even the lightest of breezes.

Last Years of the Dynasty

John G. Rathborne led his firm towards the beckoning twentieth

century with a firm hand. During the 1870s he started to develop
the market-garden potential of the lands at Dunsinea in order that
farm work would be available for all workers during slack periods in
the trade. As a result, until its move to East Wall, the firm was able
to provide year-round work for its employees. In 1880, with a view
to keeping the firm on a sound economic footing, he registered the
business name of John G. Rathborne. The legal matters relating to
the registration were finalised by his brother Henry Baily
Rathborne. Henry Baily died on 26 June 1885 aged seventy-one
years; he was buried in the family vault in Castleknock on 30 June.
Around this time John's son Henry Burnley Rathborne entered
Trinity College, Dublin, where he completed his MA studies. In
1887 John leased three parcels of land involving a total of 'forty-
nine acres, one rood and twenty eight perches, Irish plantation
measures, from John Trant Hamilton, JP, Abbottstown House,
Castleknock, at an annual rent of £469=10s=9d late Irish currency,
equivalent to £433=8s=5d present currency (sterling)'. The
agreement was entered in the Registry of Deeds on 17 May 1887. It
was around this time that John, approaching the age of seventy,
devoted almost all his energies to further developing the family
farm (probably the reason for leasing further land from his
neighbour) and restricted his commitments to the candle business,
giving full control of the firm's day-to-day affairs to his only child,
Henry B. Two years later, on 29 April 1889, John was shaken by the
death of his cousin, W.H. Rathborne, son of William and Penelope.
W.H. lived nearby in Scripplestown and was very much a part of
everyday family life.

Henry B. was, like his father, a barrister by profession and later a
Justice of the Peace; he was also very interested in church affairs,
and on 14 April 1903 he was elected Peoples' Church Warden to St
Brigid's. Henry B. had taken an active interest in the trade since the
age of ten. On 27 October 1897 he married Mary Jane Florence,
eldest daughter of Charles Robert Barton of Waterfoot, County
Fermanagh. He continued to live at Dunsinea. That he was indeed
in full control of the business is proved by the articles mentioned in
the settlement of marriage between Henry B. and Florence, which

refers to 'wax and spermaceti candle manufacturer and oil refiner at Dunsinea, County Dublin and Essex Street, Dublin'. Florence was related to Robert Barton, elected to the Dáil in the 1918 General Election as Sinn Féin candidate for County Wicklow (West). He was one of the signatories of the 1921 Treaty, which led to the foundation of the Irish Free State, and he voted in its favour in the Dáil division of 7 January 1922. Florence was also related to Pam Barton, a pre-World War II England Ladies' Golf Champion who joined the WRAF at the start of the war and was killed when the RAF warplane she was piloting from its factory of manufacture to its designated military airfield crash-landed in the Thames estuary.

By the late 1800s the plant at Ashtown was getting old and in the early 1890s there were a number of fires in the storehouse. Besides the age of the plant, another feature that did not help in the area of fire safety was the fact that the firm still clung to its age-old tradition of lighting the entire complex – production area, stores and offices – by candlelight. Disaster struck in the summer of 1895 when a very serious fire swept through the factory causing great damage. No record of a call-out by the Dublin Fire Brigade can be found and it is possible that the fire had burnt itself out – a lady who had four generations of her family working at Dunsinea maintains that this is indeed what happened. Soon after the fire the works were rebuilt and the trade continued. However, quite a lot of documentation relating to the history of the business and family was lost in the blaze, including title deeds, letters, invoices and wages ledgers.

John G. Rathborne died on Saturday 23 March 1895, aged 76. He was buried on 26 March 1895 in the family vault at St Brigid's Churchyard. The burial ceremony was performed by his lifelong friend and pastor, Rev. Ralph Sadlier. Sadlier officiated at nearly all Rathborne family births, marriages and deaths until his own death, in Geneva, on 28 September 1902, aged eighty-eight. Under John's will, which was dated 9 September 1890 and which went to probate on 2 August 1895, his son Henry B. inherited the business and family home at Dunsinea.

Kate Florence, mentioned earlier as the favourite of Rowan

Hamilton, outlived all her family and spent her later years in the luxurious ambience of Fitzwilliam Square, where she lived to the age of eighty-seven. She died on 17 August 1900 and was the last of the Rathbornes to be buried in the family vault at St Brigid's. The burial service was carried out on 22 August by Rev. R.B. Redding. The family vault is still there, situated beside the main entrance to the church. An interesting anecdote relates to the remains of a bullet lodged in the granite structure of the vault and clearly visible. Canon Paul Colton, Rector at St Brigid's, states that this happened in 1919, when two local men returned from the Great War and smuggled a gun into the country. They went to the graveyard one night and indulged in some target-practice, using the headstones to test their marksmanship. One of the bullets lodged in the Rathborne tomb. The men were never apprehended, for in those days the church was surrounded by fields and the village was a sleepy hamlet many miles outside the city boundary, which then ended at Phibsborough.

Henry B. and Florence had two sons, Henry Barton (nicknamed Barty by all who knew him), born on 4 February 1899, and Charles John Errol, born in 1902, and it was this generation which saw the severing of the Rathborne family's connection with candle-making. Henry B. had initially intended Barty to inherit the company but his young son declined, being of the view that 'candles are on the way out and electricity is on the way in'. (Though Errol was only twelve at this time and was probably too young to form any opinions, Eileen Chambers, who worked at the factory in 1920, recalls being told by Charlie English that the young Errol showed 'no interest or passion whatever in his father's chosen profession'.) Barty's view that there was no future in candle manufacturing was by no means unique at the time, for in those days the star of electricity was rising – cities had converted to public electric lighting and the huge passenger liners, the *Titanic* and the *Olympic*, did not have any candlelight fittings used in their construction, highlighting the brave new world of electric power. (Rathborne's are currently marketing their *Titanic* brand of traditional beeswax candles in packets of six, which retail from US$23 in the USA. It is possible that Rathborne candles were used in the famous vessel's chapel.)

The company entered the twentieth century in a strong trading position, dominating the domestic Irish market. In March 1909 the firm was authorised to use the Irish Trade Mark on all their goods and the Certificate of Authorisation for its use was issued by the Irish Industrial Development Association on 18 March 1909. Henry B. ensured that the 'Dánta in Éirinn' symbol appeared on all their products, and the company also used the symbol in their advertising literature. Henry B. remained at the helm at Dunsinea, but being unable to get his sons interested in the industry he sold his interest in the firm to John Barrington & Sons Limited, a subsidiary of the giant Lever group, on 18 March 1914. Shortly afterwards he sold Dunsinea House and divested himself of the adjoining lands, which had been closely associated with the Rathborne family name since 1744. He went to live in County Fermanagh, the birthplace of his wife. It appears he left Dublin shortly after selling the business, for the last mention of him in *Thom's Directory* is in the 1914 edition. In 1920, with his wife Florence, he settled in 'Blen-Na-Lung', an estate situated five miles due east of Beleek and near Castlecaldwell. Florence died on 20 February 1932 and Henry B. lived on at 'Blen-Na-Lung' until his death on 27 August 1943.

Barty Rathborne graduated from Sandhurst and served in the British Army in India with the Second Dorsetshire Regiment. In the early 1920s he took up photography in London, where he met his wife Louisa Florence, eldest daughter of Sidney Herbert Moore, of Richmond, Surrey, whom he married in 1932. He came to Ireland with Louie in 1934, following his mother's death, and moved into 'Blen-na-Lung' with his father, where he and Louie lived until 1975 when the estate was sold. They then moved into a house about five miles away and shortly after that Barty suffered a mild stroke. He died in March 1982 and was survived by Louie, who on 12 April 1998 celebrated her ninety-third birthday.

Charles John Erroll Rathborne was educated in England, at St Lawrence College in Hastings and at Sandhurst. He settled in England and in the early 1920s he took up a job offer from the tea

Louie Rathborne
(PHOTO BRENDAN FAUGHNAN)

merchants J. Lyons & Co. Ltd. He spent his working life with the company, becoming an eminent tea-taster; he was also a director of the firm for many years prior to his retirement from active life. He married Vida, daughter of Edward Ernest Mayor Hett, of Aldwickbury, Harpenden, Herts. When he retired he purchased a large dairy farm, located not far from Cheltenham, where he lived until his death on 28 May 1974. During his lifetime he obviously cast an eye on his father's former business from time to time, for during a debate in the letters pages of the London *Sunday Times* in late 1945 as to the identity of the oldest European manufacturing firm in continuous production he wrote to the editor on the matter. His letter, signed C.J.E. Rathborne, Rickmansworth, was published on 21 October 1945 and read as follows:

> Sir – The chandler's firm referred to by your correspondent Mr. Brian Routledge is undoubtedly my late father's business, Messrs J.G. Rathborne and Sons at Dunsinea, Castleknock, Co. Dublin, established in 1488. It was founded by a Lancastrian ancestor who received a grant of land in Ireland in recognition of his services to Henry VII in the Wars of the Roses. The firm passed from father to son until 1912 when it was bought by Messrs Lever Brothers. Since then it has changed hands on one or two occasions. The factory has been transferred to East Wall Road, Dublin, where it is still in production.

Erroll's letter contains more folklore than fact in the reference to the grant of land in Ireland. The first recorded land ownership in

Machine-candle section, Dunsinea, c.1896

Master wax chandler, Dunsinea, c.1896

the name of a Rathborne was a small parcel of ground in the Liberties area of Dublin city – hardly a gift or favour from a grateful King for loyal services rendered.

John G. Rathborne & Company Limited

Using the original firm's registered business name of John G. Rathborne, the factory continued to operate at Ashtown, satisfying markets at home, in England, Scotland and Wales and in the colonies of the British Empire. Barrington & Sons continued the Rathborne tradition and provided some farm work during off-peak production periods. The new owners drew up the Articles of Association of the company on 28 March 1914 and three days later it was incorporated under the Companies Acts 1908/13 as John G. Rathborne & Company Limited. The objects of the Company were 'to acquire, take over as a going concern the business now carried on in Dublin by Henry Burnley Rathborne trading as John G. Rathborne.' On 31 March 1914 the new shareholders were registered in the Companies Office, Dublin, as follows: Jonathan Pim Barrington, 12 Morehampton Road and Director of John Barrington & Sons Limited, 8000 shares; Joseph Edward Robinson, 33 Home Farm Road and Director of John Barrington & Sons Limited, 4000 shares; Stanley Kay Sloan, Dunsinea, Castleknock, Director of John G. Rathborne, one share; Dermot Reilly Sidford, Avalon, Sutton, Company Secretary and Director of John G. Rathborne, one share.

Stanley Kay Sloan had been employed as Works Manager by Henry Burnley Rathborne at Dunsinea and remained in that position under the new owners. He resided at Dunsinea until it was disposed of by the company sometime in 1927, when he moved to Clontarf. Dermot Reilly Sidford had been employed by Henry B. as Office Manager in Essex Street and he too was retained; both men remained with the company until their retirement – for Sloan this was in March 1946, after spending his whole working life with the firm. Likewise Reilly Sidford retired as managing director of the firm the following year, again after spending his full working life with Rathborne's.

Dermot Reilly Sidford and H.E. McCormick in Bray, Co. Wicklow,
on a company outing, 1955

The premises at 44 Essex Street and 1-3 Crampton Court 'adjacent to the Empire Palace Theatre' (the Olympia) were vacated, thus ending nearly two hundred years of continuous occupation by the Rathborne family. *Thom's Directory* of 1917 lists both premises as vacant. The house at 44 Essex Street still stands and has not been altered much since it was first occupied by Rathborne's. Indeed, a visit to the building recently showed little sign of major interior alterations, and the old, beautiful wooden banisters were highlighted by the glass skylight in the roof. The premises is now owned by Temple Bar Properties Limited, and the former Rathborne workshops and stores at the rear, at Crampton Court, are presently just a small cluster of ruins.

Rathborne's continued trading during the difficult years of the War of Independence (1918–21) and during the ensuing Civil War and the breakdown in law and order that followed. The district saw a considerable amount of activity during these years. Indeed, Ashtown Cross, not far from the factory at Dunsinea, was the site of an IRA ambush on the official car of Lord French, the English Lord Lieutenant, on Friday 19 December 1919. Four years later the Troubles were brought right to the door of the candle factory at Dunsinea.

Robbery Under Arms

The beautiful, serene work atmosphere in the rural setting of Dunsinea was broken on 19 October 1923 when the candle factory was the scene of an armed robbery. Three men, armed with guns, burst into the factory and went straight to the wages office. There they forced staff to hand over the money. However, only forty-three pounds was taken, as the firm, adapting to the Troubles, had taken to handling their financial affairs with caution and paid their staff on a rota basis every working day, which meant that at any given time there would not be a substantial amount of cash on the premises. The raiders took their cash and fled. Eileen Chambers (née Kinsella), who lived in the gate lodge at the Ashtown entrance to the Phoenix Park, worked with the firm from 1920 to 1930. She now lives in Marino and recalls that fateful day:

> I was in the toilets with my friend when we heard a commotion outside. When we came out I heard Charlie English saying 'they won't get away with this' and he and Willie Coates, who lived on the Navan Road, ran out after them. Charlie got on his bicycle and chased after the robbers. He followed them as far as Glass's Garage. When the police caught up Charlie told them he saw the robbers going in the direction of Keaveen churchyard. Though the robbers had travelled some distance, it appears that they were running around in a circle, for when they stopped to count the proceeds of the robbery they were only a few fields away from the factory. The police caught them in a gap in the hedge on the roadside dividing out the money. They arrested them and put them in the police car, where one of the robbers produced a gun and shot one of the policemen dead. He then ran away over the fields with a second robber while the third remained seated in the police car. The police gave chase and in an exchange of gunfire the armed robber was shot dead. The other two were tried by a military court shortly after that and the one who stayed put in the police car received a

prison sentence while the other was sentenced to death and executed by firing squad the day following the trial. Charlie English received a citation from the Irish Free State for his bravery in chasing after the robbers and was presented with a small monetary reward.

Eileen's account of the robbery is confirmed by the newspapers of the time and from records in the Garda Museum, Dublin Castle. The Company wrote to Commandant Moynihan, CID, Oriel House, Dublin, offering their condolences at the loss of his colleague, on the day after the raid. On 9 November 1923 Stanley Sloan wrote to Charlie English as follows:

> At a meeting of Directors held yesterday I was instructed to express to you their appreciation of your action in so promptly following the men who raided the factory on the 19th October, and by your doing so materially assisted the cause of law and order. They further instruct me to hand you the enclosed as a practical recognition of the valuable service you then rendered.

A note which the firm sent to its parent Candles Limited in London – which had bought Rathborne's only that year – also refers to the robbery:

> On 19th October 1923 three armed men entered our Factory and held up the Office staff and they took the sum of £43.19.9d. They were disappointed that they did not get all the weekly wages, but thanks to the precautions which we have been taking for some time, i.e. changing the day and time of paying, they missed the major portion of the wages. The three men were captured shortly after the robbery, there was some shooting and one of the raiders died from a bullet wound and another is under sentence of death for the murder of one of the Detective Officers who arrested them, and the third has been sentenced to a term of imprisonment. Most of the stolen money was recovered, the balance will be paid by the Insurance Company.

Eileen Chambers remembers

Eileen Chambers was a typical Rathborne employee, living within the environs of the factory. She recalls how she started with the firm:

> Five friends called to my door one day to tell me Mr. Sloan was taking on some girls up at the candle factory and I went with them – Kathleen Redmond and Nellie Mahon from Roosevelt Cottages on the corner of Navan and Nephin Roads, Mary Kerrigan from Mooney's lodge, Cabra Cross, Nellie Brown who lived in the grounds of the Viceregal Lodge, Phoenix Park, and Annie Dodd, St Joseph's Cottages, Blackhorse Lane. We all got a job there and then, and I started in the Packing Department on twenty-seven shillings a week. It was good wages compared to working behind the counter in a sweet shop for eight shillings a week. I lived in the gate lodge at Ashtown Gate and everybody around worked in Dunsinea – three of the Horans, Whacker Little and the big and small Mattie Daly from Blackhorse Lane. Generations of the Little family worked in Rathborne's. Dada Little, the father of James Little, used to stand at his gate and tell us fascinating stories of Rathborne's, candle-making, the local area, the Blackhorse Tavern and in particular the Famine and the effects that it had on Blackhorse Lane life. He often talked about the people on the lane who died during the famine. A number of men joined the British Army and fought in World War I. After that war a few of the residents on the lane died during the great 'flu of 1919. The Manager, Mr Sloan, was there at seven o'clock every morning. I remember too that Mrs Smith, who lived in the area of the factory, brought an aluminium container full of food into the fields to feed her family, as she wanted them to eat their food out in the fresh air.

When the transfer to East Wall was made, Eileen 'walked from Ashtown Gate down to Parkgate Street to catch the ten-past-seven tram to Ballybough, then walked down the East Wall Road to be in work for ten minutes to eight, every morning'. She found the new location

> very exposed – the sea breeze would take the nose off you. In 1926 I bought a bicycle in McHugh Himself in Talbot Street for two-and-sixpence a week and then cycled into work every day until I left the firm upon getting married in August 1930. … Mr. Sloan's nickname was Slicker and he was a very kind man, but was also a shy, retiring person. His son became a Harley Street doctor and his wife's brother lived in the Observatory at Dunsink.

Eileen Chambers,
Rathborne employee 1921–30
(PHOTO BERNARD NEARY)

Eileen enjoyed good working conditions for the time, which included a staff canteen and a doctor on call. She bought a crown loaf for 2d and a knob of butter for 1d for her lunch in the canteen. Her working life was spent with all the people whose families had given generations of craftsmen and women to Rathborne's: the Dodds, Browns, Mooneys, Littles, Englishes, Horans, Dalys and Smiths. Some of these families are still represented in the area; for example, there are Dalys, Dodds, Horans and Reids presently living on Blackhorse Avenue, from where, through the centuries, Rathborne's drew a considerable body of their workers.

Houses, Lands and Factory Disposal

Dunsinea Manor was built in 1744 by William Rathborne. Through time the house became part of the manufacturing works complex. After the entire property was sold in the mid-1920s the house passed into the hands of numerous owners; the current owner of

Dunsinea Manor is Aidan Prior, who purchased the premises in 1962 and has lived there ever since. By coincidence, Aidan designed candles for the company during the 1950s. Nursing a deep appreciation of the history surrounding him, Aidan has expertly and proudly unearthed every bit of evidence of bygone days, as well as retaining the original integrity of the historic house both inside and outside.

The remains of a kiln can be seen to the present day just outside Dunsinea Manor. There are remains of ceramic tiles under the present-day flagstones and there is also evidence of the existence of a vat in the car-park now attached to the manor house. Some pipe-remains attaching to the residence bear out the existence of old plant machinery and testify to the fact that some small-scale candle manufacturing took place within the domestic residence, probably during periods of peak demand. The house, in cut stone and nestled in mature surroundings which include centuries-old listed trees, is worthy of an An Taisce listing. It is in excellent repair and holds promise as a future museum and treasure of the nation.

Rathborne's leased a house, offices and gate lodge to Henry

Aidan Prior, present guardian of Dunsinea Manor, points to the remains of a kiln.
(PHOTO BERNARD NEARY)

McDermott in 1919 and part of the factory buildings and site passed into the hands of Denis Ferns in 1920. In the early 1920s, following the relocation of Rathborne's to East Wall, the old factory and some land was leased by Mrs Ferns, the wife of Denis Ferns, to James J. Doherty Limited. In 1928 the factory was occupied by Industrial Minerals of Ireland Limited. In 1948 the factory was leased, again from the Ferns family, by Powers Products Limited. In later years there were a number of occupants, until Croda Paints established their business there in the 1960s. They are now part of Manders Coatings and Inks, who are the current occupiers of the former factory site and some lands. There is now little evidence of the Rathborne occupation at Dunsinea, apart from the remains of a furnace chimney and kiln and a boarded-up storehouse which was built in the 1770s and used in the early 1900s for storing stocks of candles.

Recent History

The purchasers of Rathborne's in 1914, John Barrington & Sons Limited, were well-known Dublin merchants and manufacturers with business premises at 201/2 Parnell Street, Dublin – then Great Britain Street – next door to Williams & Woods, the confectioners. The company director of Rathborne's, Jonathan Pim Barrington, was a son of John Barrington and he resided on Morehampton Road, Donnybrook. *Thom's Directory* of 1868 lists John Barrington & Son as 'Chandlers & Oil Merchants'; the company was a subsidiary of the huge Lever Group and was already familiar to the trade of oils and candles upon their takeover of Rathborne's. Ownership of Rathborne's was subsequently transferred to another Lever subsidiary, E. Ryan & Company, sometime prior to 1920. In 1923 the London-based Candles Limited, a subsidiary of the Shell petroleum group, bought Rathborne's from E. Ryan & Company. The audited accounts of John G. Rathborne Limited for the six months ending 30 June 1923 confirms this fact, with a sum of £3948-15-7 cited as 'Balance Lever Brothers Divestment A/c' and a sum of £125 written back into the accounts 'in accordance with instructions from Messrs Candles Ltd'.

The accounts, signed by Stokes Brothers & Pim, Chartered Accountants, make interesting reading, and show that on the 30 June 1923 the authorised share capital was £15,000 in ordinary £1 shares of which £12,002 had issued; creditors totalled £6479=1=8d; in addition the firm owed a total of £687=6=7 to John Barrington and Sons Limited and £4573=12=0d to the National Bank Limited by way of an outstanding loan. The value of company assets was as follows: leasehold property £5400; plant and machinery £3338; horses and floats £369=12=11d; debtors (less discounts) £5306=18=9d; certified stock £17,351=9=4d, cash in hand £42=9=8d. In addition a War Office Claim for £320 was inserted into the company accounts. Payments from the accounts for the six-month period included bank interest of £81=14=9d; interest on loans £66=4=0d; pensions £20=16=0d; legal and accountancy fees £8=10=0d; rent and rates £67=13=10, legal and accountancy fees £8=10=0 and advertising fees £6=5=9. The interim dividend to 31 December 1921 totalled £9732=19=0d and the profit for the first six months totalled £5788=10=11d (the full year's trading profit was £4302=3=9, so the candle industry was still quite a profitable one for the firm). Subsequently the Irish & British Petroleum Company – whose name appears in the Companies Office records for 1927 as Shell and BP [Irish Free State] Limited and in the 1938 records as Irish Shell and BP (Dublin) Limited – became known as Irish Shell.

A record from Rathborne's files for this benchmark year in the firm's history shows that a *Factory Report Monthly* was sent to the head office of Candles Limited at Leadenhall Street, London EC 3. The report, dated 14 November 1923, bears the reference SKS – Stanley K. Sloan, the Works Manager at Dunsinea – and reads as follows:

> During the month there were neither accidents to workers nor to machinery. We received three machines from the Millbay Soap & New Patent Candle Co Ltd, for making S6s, and these have been erected and are being worked to their utmost capacity. We now have adopted the method of sealing the parcels of candles with glue in both candle-making houses and find the change is an

Ashtown Cross, c.1948. Note memorial to Martin Savage in centre of green.
Dunsinea and Rathborne lands in centre background.

improvement on the old method. The change was accomplished fairly smoothly.

The girls wrapping up candles are improving in speed, they have not yet got up the speed that we hope they will eventually get with practice and when they grasp the fact that the more candles they wrap up the more money they can earn. We have made special trucks for carrying the packed cases from the wrapping-up benches and these help to minimise the amount of handling. We are experimenting with other pattern trucks for bringing the loose candles to the wrapping-up benches also with a view to saving handling.

Jonathan Pim Barrington died in May 1924 and he was replaced as director of Rathborne's by Ernest Robert Jordison, of Temora, Booterstown, Co. Dublin. On 7 January 1926 Ernest Jordison

resigned and was replaced by Charles William Murphy, Johnstown House, Chapelizod, Co. Dublin, who was then the general manager of the Irish & British Petroleum Company. This was the first recorded entry of the name of the oil company in the records of the Companies Registration Office, although from the report above to Candles Limited, and from the company's audited balance sheet account for the six month period to 30 June 1923, it had an interest in Rathborne's from that year.

Candles Limited, as the new owners of Rathborne's, signed an agreement with E. Ryan & Company Limited on 16 July 1924 in which its parent, the Lever Group, transferred the goodwill of all its illuminants and lubricants business to the Shell group subsidiary. Under that agreement the Lever Group undertook not to engage in any aspect of the illuminants industry world-wide while Candles Limited, its parent and any subsidiary, undertook not to engage in the soap or glycerin business 'anywhere in the world'. There had been intense commercial rivalry between the two groups over each one's involvement in the other's core business – Lever's soap and Shell's candles and oils – and the agreement brought the matter to a mutual settlement. Subsequently Candles Limited invested considerably in buildings and machinery, an investment which helped steer the company through the difficult trading years to follow – with the construction of the Ardnacrusha electricity-generating station on the River Shannon near Limerick in 1928 and the subsequent electrification of the country, seriously depressing the firm's domestic candlelight market. However, innovation and hard work, coupled with investment and expansion, helped the firm to survive and later prosper in the industry.

In the contracting candle market of the 1920s, rationalisation became necessary and the company decided to move the works at Ashtown and registered office at Parnell Street to one central location in the city, at the storage area at East Wall, leased nearly sixty years previously, in 1866, by John G. Rathborne. In late 1924 work began on the construction of a modern factory on the site of the Dublin Petroleum Stores and the following year the firm moved into its new premises and disposed of the factory and lands at Dunsinea, thus closing a long chapter on the history of John G. Rathborne Limited. The transfer was made during the summer of 1925 and the change of registered office to East Wall Road was notified to the Companies Office on 25 November 1925.

Two years after the firm moved to its new factory on East Wall Road, Stanley Kay Sloan left the old Rathborne home, which was then sold by the company, and took up residence in Clontarf. It is quite interesting to note that until it was vacated in 1927, the fine period cut-stone house, in keeping in line with family and company tradition, was also (like the factory premises at Dunsinea) still entirely illuminated by candlelight.

(PHOTO BRENDAN FOGARTY)

Sales & Merchandising staff, 1998
Back row, l. to r.: *Joan Cunningham, Gavin Clarke, Pauline Joyce, Carl Roche, Justin Kneeshaw, Nan Veale, David Buggy, Michael Duffy*
Front row, l. to r.: *Terry Roche, Peadar Lennon, Carmel O'Leary, Louise Fitzgibbon*

Boxing room, Dunsinea, c.1896

Machine candles, Dunsinea, c.1890. Note wood panelling in background

CHAPTER THREE

Dunsinea Village and Garden Factory

Speaking to the many, many people whose families have been for generations connected to Rathborne's would leave one in no doubt that the company was indeed a village, a place where everyone knew everyone else and where life was pleasant and agreeable. The candle factory – known as the Phoenix Candle Works – was located in close proximity to the Rathborne family home of 'Dunsinea Manor'. A lane-way, walled on both sides and with shading foliage, led off the road into a cul-de-sac incorporating the factory yard. There was a back exit from the family residences and from another residence, which housed the works manager, into the factory grounds. It may be assumed that the factory took its name from the Phoenix Park, less than a mile away from the Ashtown Gate. It is worth noting that when the factory was located on Pill Lane in 1636, one of the streets nearby was called Phoenix Street.

The main approach to the candle works was via the present-day Navan Road, then called the New Road, going down the boreen at Ashtown Cross that led down to the Tolka river. The approach changed somewhat with the construction of the Royal Canal and in the time of William Rathborne the workers passed over Longford Bridge, constructed in 1792, and then down a country road past woodland slopes bordering the meandering Tolka, which was crossed by a rustic single-arch stone bridge, on their way to work. From 1850, in the time of John G. Rathborne, their path brought them past little Ashtown railway station. It was a picturesque setting, described in the *Irish Industrial Journal* in 1910 as follows:

> When our representative visited Rathborne's candle factory the country-side revealed patches of light green aftergrass, shining through the glorious timber which abounds in the demesne. Here indeed is a garden factory, surrounded on all sides by great clusters of elms and beeches. The very walls are covered with flowers and the portals are decked with shrubs. In the centre of the demesne stands a Georgian mansion, behind which is a garden sheltered by a plantation of trees which flank the out-houses which open on to the factory building which are exceedingly airy and lightsome and surrounded by cheerful vistas. This serenity of country life is united to the pursuit of a lucrative manufacturing business.

The site of the old candle factory, modernised and redeveloped in recent years, is now occupied by Manders Coatings & Inks (formerly Croda Inks Ireland Limited). Here one finds another coincidence – Ernest O'Connor, who presently works with Manders, recalls that his father John O'Connor was a general worker in Rathborne's for over fifty years and started out on his working life in the rural setting of the Phoenix Candle Works. When John O'Connor retired in November 1955 he brought to a close a family service record of 165 years combined tenure with the company, as his father and grandfather before him also worked at Rathborne's. Ernest recalls his father's service in the candle industry:

> It is strange to think that I am working in the very place where my father, grandfather and great-grandfather started their working lives. My father was on the full-time payroll of Rathborne's and he was also one of those workers who were given farm work in the fields just beside us there when candle-making was slack. He often told us stories about the factory here, horses that pulled

the carts with the finished product, the great fire of 1895 and the quiet rural work setting and about the old Rathborne family.

The Rathborne homes, factory and farm were situated adjacent to the Observatory at Dunsink. The developers of the Observatory purchased an estate of over fourteen acres in order to ensure that speculative builders would not put up houses to block the views from their telescopes. They were thus able to enjoy unrestricted views – until 1882, when it was found that the transit of the planet Venus across the sun's disc, an event that will next happen in the year 2004, would be 'hidden by a tree growing in the garden of our neighbour, Mr. Rathborne'. Fortunately, according to the records of the Observatory, 'Mr. Rathborne was obliging enough to fell the tree and the transit was observed through a providential break in the clouds.'

Henry Burnley Rathborne – Factory Tour Guide

Following the launch of the 17,900-ton battleship *Dreadnought* in 1906 – then the biggest in the world and which took just a year and a day to complete – Germany and England became locked in a spiralling arms race. A terrible world war was on the horizon, but at the Rathborne chandlery at Ashtown the quiet life continued. To get an insight into what the candle industry at Dunsinea was like at this time, the reader should let his or her mind wander back to the close of that first decade of the twentieth century. Imagine the refined persona of the proprietor of the Phoenix Candle Works, Henry Burnley Rathborne, welcoming you to the rural setting at Dunsinea, and bringing you on a tour of the factory complex and the wax-drying fields in the heat of a beautiful summer in the year of 1910:

'Welcome to the Phoenix Candle Works, where the firm of John G. Rathborne have been engaged in the craft of candle-making for over 150 years, though we have been in the industry here in Ireland for over 420 years. I will commence the tour by showing the old process of making candles, which used to be mainly composed of spermaceti. Now a blend of other materials is usually mixed with it for ordinary lighting. Here is the long oil-house where large quantities of spermaceti are stored, and this is where you will notice the international character of the Irish candle trade, with the Arctic Ocean and the Sea of Okhotsk being ransacked to provide materials for Irish candles.

'Spermaceti is a substance procured from whales and this is a sample which has just arrived from Japan, where there are important whale fisheries. The spermaceti is an oily, glutinous substance which yields the familiar sperm machine oil. It is found in two or three varieties of the sea-monster, notably in the bottle-nosed whale. A very good sperm is also found in the cachelot or southern species. It was during the first half of the eighteenth century that it was discovered that candles could be made from this oil, which is present in the head cavities of sperm whales. One ordinary-sized whale would yield nearly one ton of spermaceti in a crude state, which is put into cloth bags and placed under a

Staff of John G. Rathborne Ltd, 1997

hydraulic press to remove all the oil. The pressure of ninety tons is so great that canvas bags will not stand it and accordingly the spermaceti is placed in horse-hair bags and comes out in solid cakes of great firmness, which are then broken into pieces and boiled in water to separate the impurities. Upon cooling the spermaceti is again boiled in water in these troughs, but this time with a weak solution of potash to remove the remaining oil. The resulting pure spermaceti is a hard white mass with a beautiful, flaky crystalline appearance which characterises candles made of this fine substance.

'Candles made from spermaceti burn with a white flame which is taken as the standard unit of light in photometry. The oil which we draw off during the process is sold for lubricating purposes and we use and retail it as machine oil. I might say that our sperm test here in Ashtown is remarkably high – it has often been wondered, until analysed and proved, how we could produce spermaceti of so high a melting point. Spermaceti candles are made in moulds and are quite expensive, being only slightly cheaper than wax candles. Two native whaling stations have opened up in Ireland in the past couple of years, one at Inniskee and the other at Belmullet. They caught about six sperm whales last year but I did not succeed in getting one. They have, however, promised to advise me of their next catch and then I hope to make Irish spermaceti candles from Irish-caught whales.

'We now pass into the Paraffin Candle Department. Nowadays candles are made mostly from shale scales – a material that comes from the United States of America. The paraffin wax is melted down in the steam jacket-pans just here. There are, as you can see, several apartments full of the most up-to-date machines for making candles. These resemble American organs in appearance, each one containing a number of moulds, and cold water is circulated around them until cooled. The candles are driven out of the moulds by a simple lever, the wick being automatically fed through the wax. These compound machines, as we call them, make no less than three hundred candles at a time. Take a close look at the paraffin wax; of course it is not the sole component of the common candle, for a composition made of stearine is used – or should I say blended

– with it. Stearine is a fatty substance which we import from France and Belgium.

'Though this month, July, is an off-month in the trade, you can see that the frames are all full of wax, and all around us there are countless rows of candles. Now as we go into the Packing Department, many hands are sorting and arranging the candles with a rattle-like revolver practice – we are enjoying one of our best years ever. The size of machine candles made here varies from those weighing one-over-seventy-two of a pound to those of six-and-a-quarter pounds each. As I have said, the firm has never had such a demand at this time of the year and we are quite as busy as if it were winter. I attribute this in most part to the current industrial revival – a dozen years ago we at Rathborne's could hardly venture to offer our goods as native manufacture but now the call is for Irish candles and Irish candles only. It is actually a good time to be in business in Ireland. Every factory is most industrious and the country is in the grips of prosperity – even as we speak they are working on a huge passenger liner in Belfast, called the *Olympic*, which is being launched in the autumn. A second liner, a huge vessel which they intend to call the *Titanic*, is under construction – a fine indication of the health of the industrial life of the country at present.

'Prepare your nostrils for a truly magnificent odour, for we are now entering the lofty and lightsome apartment where the charming scent of honey fills the air. This is where we make the big, wax church-altar candles – the aspect of the chandlery manufacture for which my firm is, perhaps, most celebrated in this part of the world, and we send candles for religious ritual purposes to England, Scotland and Wales as well as throughout Ireland and of course to the colonies. However, we also supply good-quality beeswax candles to those markets for domestic consumption. Great Britain is by far our most important market after the home market and the present consumption there is about 54,000 tons per annum. We export some products to the European mainland and in this regard it is worthy to note that we supply some of the Greek churches.

'The beeswax we use here at the Phoenix Candle Works comes from France, Belgium, Madagascar, Mombasa and even from The

Gambia, on the west coast of Africa. The Gambia wax is used in large quantities. I would use Irish beeswax, which is a good all-round wax for bleaching and working with, but there is just not a very large supply of it. The modern method of section hives was intended for the production of honey for consumption but the old straw hives were better for yielding wax suitable to candle-manufacturing. Beeswax is obtained from honeycomb by a simple process of melting and straining to remove impurities; this yields a yellow wax with an unmistakable smell of honey. The quantity of beeswax which we purchase during the year is considerable. As you can see, the wax church-altar candles are made by hand, being rolled on a marble slab. We make them as high as 100 per cent pure beeswax, although the present standard qualities are 75 and 65 per cent pure beeswax. The passage at the end of the wax apartment leads into the chamber for making tapers from cotton, which you can see is run in reels through a standard bath of wax.

'From this aromatic apartment we can exit directly into the bleaching fields, which represented the old industry as first established here at Ashtown. It is actually a garden here and you can see stretched in front of you vast layers of beeswax on long table-troughs. After being melted the beeswax is poured over a drum which is kept revolving in a water-trough so that it comes off in shavings which float on the water. These shavings are then laid out in the open on linen cloths and exposed to the sun for several weeks to bleach. There is also a method of bleaching by chemicals but my firm relies entirely on the sun, the wax being untouched by chemical. This gives a much better result in the burning of the candles and the constitution of the wax. Ireland is a good country for bleaching though many do not know it – the alternation of sun and damp is exactly what is wanted. It is the same in the manufacture of linen. We pride ourselves in this unique bleaching process which has enhanced our reputation across the water and throughout the Colonies.

'I have mentioned linen – well, in olden times my grandfather and great-grandfather used to send Irish linen to Spain in exchange for Spanish beeswax. Wax is a valuable commodity and the present price is between £140 and £150 a ton. It would be well if our bee-keepers turned their attention to producing a steady supply of Irish wax for there is a ready market always available for it. Lastly, we also produce a high-quality sealing wax, which is filled off on frames in a special department. Just off the bleaching yards is the boxing shed. Here our carpenters make the boxes from Irish wood which are used in packing our candles for dispatch to the trade. So you can see that we use native resources here at Ashtown wherever possible. In my forefathers' days you were very important in the trade if you manufactured wax candles. Indeed, according to Campbell, author of *The London Tradesman*, published in 1747, the business of the wax chandler was "more profitable than that of tallow chandler and reckoned a more genteel trade". Wax candle manufacturing is still more profitable than any other form of production.

'Our firm held the contract for lighting Dublin city in former days, but you must accept that candles would not suffice in these degenerate times. A number of generations of Rathbornes were involved in the contract to supply public candle-lighting to the city of Dublin. Of course, the development of gas lighting in England by William Murdock, whose ideas foresaw many later developments in gas lighting, led to the demise of this particular market. Did you know that the cotton mill in Manchester, in which William Murdock installed one thousand gas lights, was at one stage supplied with candles from this firm? The records proving this were lost in a severe fire in the wax-candle store-room fifteen years ago but my father told me that we had supplied that cotton-mill almost one hundred years ago, in 1810. It was the 1850s by the time gas lighting and the kerosene lamp, with its flat, woven wick and glass chimney, came into common use and considerably diminished our industrial-based candle-user's custom. However, the ever-increasing populations resulting from the progress of the Industrial Revolution means that we are still as busy as ever we were, and long may it continue. Do you know that the major source of lighting in many Dublin homes even today is the candle? Quite a lot of people, despite improvements in living conditions, can only afford candle power as a source of light and gas lighting in the homes of the

Rolling wax candles, Dunsinea, c.1896

wealthy does not extend to the upstairs apartments, where candlelight is, to a great extent, the preferred source of illumination.

'The Irish candles made in the Phoenix Candle Works have long been famous for purity and burning excellence and the results achieved prove the care with which materials are selected from the ends of the earth, gathered as they are from the frozen eternity of the Arctic wastes to the molten coasts of The Gambia and Madagascar. As a result the Irish people have no need to go outside their country for bargains as we in the Irish manufacturing industry are thoroughly alive to the requirements of modern trade. The main lines of our celebrated brands are 'Ivy Wax' and 'Irish Wax' as well as paraffin, sperm and best hard stearine candles. In recent years the firm has earned a widespread name for its excellent Carriage Candles, which are to be had in composite qualities. Candles with self-fitting ends have come generally into use and all the best qualities manufactured by us can be had in this convenient form.

'I enjoy this business very much, as indeed does every one of my workers. The work performed by us all here cannot be surpassed anywhere for the purity of materials, the care with which they are handled and the skill and perfection with which they are moulded – and it is all offered at the keenest prices in a competitive market. We are a truly Irish firm and all hands are Irish, nearly all raised in the neighbourhood, from Blackhorse Lane, the villages of Blanchardstown and Ashtown and the fields of Cabragh. It is worthy to note that almost all have been exclusively brought up to the candle trade. I will finish off by showing you into my house just over here, which I am proud to say is solely illuminated by candlelight, and we can enjoy a cup of Irish-blended tea – mind the flowers and shrubs on the way around the factory to Dunsinea Manor.'

Guaranteed Irish

The early 1900s saw a rising interest in Irish-manufactured products and Henry Burnley Rathborne was to the fore in promoting the indigenous product, be it his own firm's or that of any other Irish enterprise. He was also a great supporter of Irish trade fairs and never missed an event. In this regard it is interesting to note that Rathborne's was one of the first companies to utilize the Irish Made Trademark upon its introduction in 1907. It appears that we, as a nation, had the same inferiority complex regarding our output in those days as we had during the 1950s and 1960s, thinking that only the imported product is the quality product.

Later generations of Irish companies, business men and women, including John G. Rathborne & Co. Limited, would follow in his path, supporting government and government-funded bodies in promoting Irish industry with campaigns like the 'Buy Irish' campaign in the 1960s and later 'Guaranteed Irish' and 'Q' symbol initiatives. Henry Burnley also had the distinction of being the last member of the Rathborne clan to live in Dunsinea House, the family seat at Scribblestown.

Dunsinea House

Although not as old as Dunsinea Manor, where the first Rathborne took up residence in the district in 1763, Dunsinea House has had a very colourful history. It was built around 1811 by Henry Rathborne, whose brother William Humphrey then moved into the original family home at Dunsinea Manor, across the yard from the Phoenix Candle Works. The road leading to the houses and factory at this time was a private one, with a gate allowing access up the quiet roadway. There are records of a right of passage being given to 'John G. Rathborne and his servants etc' in 1887 by Ian Trant Hamilton of Abbottstown through what is now the road leading up to Dunsinea from the Scribblestown crossroads. It is not clear why this right of passage was needed at the time, as the families enjoyed harmonious relations and the Rathbornes owned land on both sides of the quiet roadway. The last family member to reside in Dunsinea House was Henry Burnley Rathborne. He leased it in 1912 on giving up the business and sold the house to Denis Ferns, a cattle-dealer from North King Street, Dublin, in 1919. In 1943 Margaret Ferns sold the house to a Sergeant Joseph Hancock, who sold it again in 1946.

Dunsinea House has earned a place in Irish history due to the fact that the writer Sir John Betjeman resided there. Born in Highgate, London, in 1906, he tried to join the Royal Air Force following the outbreak of the Second World War in 1939; he was unsuccessful and instead obtained a position with the Ministry of Information in the Films Division. In 1941 he was posted to Dublin as Press Attaché to Sir John Mahaffey in the British Embassy and remained here until 1943. He spent his first six months of that posting at Dunsinea House, with his wife Penelope Chetwode and their young son Paul. He did not live in isolation at Dunsinea, for his friend M.J. MacManus, the literary editor of the *Irish Press*, gave him the long-term loan of an automobile. It was not the writer's first visit to Ireland for he had been here on visits to literary friends during the 1930s. While at Dunsinea he contributed reviews to the *Dublin Magazine*, a long-running and celebrated literary magazine founded by the poet Seumus O'Sullivan. He could have been describing the bucolic countryside of the former Rathborne estate in his poem, 'Ireland with Emily', when he wrote:

> Bells are booming down the bohreens
> White the mist along the grass
> Now the Julias, Maeves and Maureens
> Move between the fields to Mass.

A doctor, Joseph Bigger, acquired Dunsinea House in 1946; he then sold it in 1951 to Constance Vickerman of Glenageary Road, Dun Laoghaire. In 1957 the house was purchased by Major the Right Honourable William Francis, 6th Baron Carew of Castletown, Celbridge. He only had it for a short time and in May 1960 An Foras Talúntais – the forerunner to Teagasc – purchased the house and some lands from Lord Carew and established its Animal Production Division headquarters there.

Packing department, Dunsinea, c.1896

Chapter Four

East Wall Road

Henry Burnley Rathborne had steered the company into the twentieth century and then handed over stewardship to outside interests. Rathborne's had survived the gradual decline of the candle industry, and some people were quite optimistic, among them P.C. Higgs and J. Kewley, who, in an article on the uses of paraffin wax in the *Times Trade & Engineering Supplement* in 1934, wrote:

> There will always be an enormous consumption of candles for religious purposes, particularly in the East. In any case the decorative, sentimental and artistic value of the candle cannot be ignored. If the world market be considered as a whole it is probable that the candle industry will continue to be a very large user of paraffin wax for many years to come.

Meanwhile at East Wall Road, all the employees continue to use the recipe of Henry Burnley Rathborne and his predecessors, employing skilled craftsmanship, hard work, dedication and pride in their labours to get their product into Irish households. The human qualities existing at the Phoenix Candle Works in 1910 passed from the secluded countryside at Dunsinea to the bustling city location of East Wall and continue to be an integral though hidden component of the manufacturing concern of John G. Rathborne and Co. Limited.

In the mid 1920s the company developed its property on East Wall Road for the establishment of a new factory, complete with dispatch and storage areas, and commenced full production there in 1925. The move heralded the end of an era in the candle-manufacturing industry, for heretofore the lulls in the business were handled by offering the idle workers employment on the family farm. By all accounts the friendly atmosphere of the Dunsinea works was transferred to East Wall. Not only was the firm a happy place to work, but the factory and its neighbours mixed well. Michael Ladrigan grew up on Merchants Road, beside the factory. He remembers when, as a little boy, he 'would often be sent up to the candle factory office to ask the man there could he oblige with a 2d stamp. They always obliged and it saved me the long walk to Cocoman's Post Office on Church Road.' He also recalled the friendly nature and interesting stories of Bill Coates, the factory caretaker.

Rathborne's managed to increase its market share in the new economic climate of the Irish Free State and prospered throughout the 1920s and 1930s. A milestone was reached in May 1930 when the firm produced its biggest-ever candle, an eight-foot-high monster that weighed 141 pounds and took a week to manufacture, hand-made by Michael Stewart. The great candle was then carried in public procession to the grounds of the Oblate church in Inchicore, for the official opening of the Irish Lourdes – a grotto with a statue of Our Lady set in a piece of rock on which Bernadette stood during the Lourdes apparitions and which was given to the religious superior at

'Tell-tale' clock, John G. Rathborne, East Wall.

Factory office, East Wall, 1928

Inchicore by Saint Bernadette's brother. The occasion was a great religious spectacle. Dr Byrne, the Roman Catholic Archbishop of Dublin, officiated, with over 1500 members of the Oblates present and 4000 'children of Mary' dressed in white dresses, blue cloaks and flowing white veils adding colour for the thousands in attendance.

A diary kept by the factory manager throws some interesting light on working conditions in the factory during these years. The following are just a few of the entries recorded:

> 3 April 1927: E. Kavanagh had to be pulled up on different times by Mr. Sloan and myself over badly made etc. candles. I am paying special attention to his making of candles.

> 5 April 1928: J. Little almost admitted he knew he put badly made candles on the wrapping benches. He has to be watched all the time.

13 April 1928: J. O'Neill pestering E. Kinsella and preventing her from working on the tapers. Kinsella pulled off O'Neill's cap and threw it from her. Both severely cautioned.

1 February 1929: M. Graeme, J. Lindsay, P. Mahon – ceased work owing to slackness in orders.

4 March 1929: From this date to 21 May 1929 J. Cox was out. He was discharged from hospital after an accident to his eye. Cause – a nail flying from under the hammer as he was nailing up at girls' benches. Hospital Mater. Paying him 12/= per week for insurance, the same monies as his wages amount to.

20 April 1929: Slow. Church room on short time – workers off Saturdays and Mondays. Stamper – two girls off on Mondays and Tuesdays. Dora Whelan was not properly gluing the ends of packets of candles and dust could get in, etc. Called her attention to it as the packets were most untidy looking.

9 May 1929: Michael O'Brien taken on as watchman.

15 October 1930: M. Stapleton got rather fond of talking – not paying attention to her work. Reprimanded.

7 February 1932: Factory working only four days per week.

9 October 1933: F. Lynch, faulty sealing of ends of packets. Three mistakes in eight days.

21 August 1933: Working five days a week, all the factory.

16 May 1934: Wm Maher Junior, Merchant's Road, Born 2/4/1918. Commenced work 22/11/32. Ceased 16/5/34. Own accord left.

As in any employment, of course, staff always enjoyed some lighter moments and an entry in a foreman's diary for 1927 highlights one such moment: 'M. Mahon, Jim and Thomas O'Neill, discovered playing football in the storeroom during the lunch-break with a paper ball. Suspended for the evening.' The ball was made of old newspaper, rolled up and tied with candlewick – an innovation which was not pursued by the management of the time.

A Break with the Past

With the outbreak of the Second World War following the assault on Polish forces at Westerplatte, near Gdansk, on 1 September 1939, the materials used by Rathborne's in the manufacture of candles began to get scarce, although it was not until 1943, with the introduction of rationing of kerosene, that production began to suffer. The firm managed to secure adequate supplies of both raw materials and imported candles from London to meet the home demand, as there was a drop in that demand due to many of the remoter communities producing their own rush-lights from rushes and waste kitchen-fat. Tommy Kenny, from Kilconnell, Ballinasloe, County Galway, recalls those days:

> Sure there were no candles to be got anywhere. That's when I seen them cut rushes. They would hang them up to dry for a week or a fortnight and then they would peel them and dip them into the kitchen fat continuously until they thickened up. After the war we got the tilly lamp and then, shortly after that, electricity.

Trading conditions were extremely harsh during the Second World War. Many statutory rules and orders were passed during the war years by the then Minister for Supplies, Seán Lemass. The manufacture, sale and purchase of animal tallows and greases was strictly controlled and regulated, and a strict licensing regime for anybody engaged in the trade was introduced. Maximum Prices Orders were introduced for animal tallows and fats, and for both home-produced and imported candles. Up to 14 December 1943 the maximum price at which candles could be sold by a retail merchant was set at 1/11d per pound avoirdupois weight, and after that date the maximum price was fixed at 1/8d per pound avoirdupois weight. Rathborne's imported candles during the war from their parent Candles Limited of Battersea, London, and these were also governed by statutory instruments. Under the Emergency

Powers (Imported Tallow Candles) (Maximum Prices) Order, 1944 (No. 203 of 1944), the maximum price at which imported tallow candles could be sold by a retail merchant was set at 2/4d per pound. Restrictions and regulation of the industry continued after the war; in March 1946 the maximum retail price for candles was set at 1/5d per pound. It was under these trying market conditions that Rathborne's carried on their age-old tradition and survived.

The closing stages of the Second World War in 1945 saw a final break with Rathborne's family and rural past in Dunsinea when both Stanley Kay Sloan and Dermot Reilly Sidford retired. These two Rathborne veterans were succeeded by Hugh Eimer McCormick and Niall Sheerin, who also spent most of their working lives with the firm. Eimer McCormick is a native of Derry city and was educated at St Columb's College. He trained as an aeronautical engineer in London and Belfast and was completely new to the candle industry when he joined the firm in March 1945 as assistant works manager:

> I saw a small ad in the *Irish Times* in Belfast and wrote away applying for the job. I was interviewed in Dublin by Stanley Kay Sloan, who was about to retire, and Dermot Sidford. They sent me to Candles Limited in London for a second interview, which was conducted by Alex Heinman, Chairman of Candles Limited. I got the job and was told that I would have to spend six months in London training. Within four weeks I was back in Dublin, in the thick of it at East Wall Road. When I took over in 1945 there were only eight people employed in the factory and twelve in the office, with the factory only working two days a week some months due to shortages of raw materials caused by the Second World War. Around this time Niall Sheerin was taken on as Sales Manager by Dermot Sidford. I remember when I was only a few months in the job I got a call from an importer inquiring whether the firm would be interested in one thousand tons of paraffin wax at £83 a ton. I asked for two thousand tons and we were in business. Some of the people I

worked with then included Bill Carney, who was
Company Secretary, Jack Entwhistle, who was an office
clerk, Tom Long, Jack Daly, who was a master candle-
maker, and Jack Reilly. Jack Reilly was works manager and
also a brilliant fitter and inventor. The two of us actually
invented a prototype automatic extrusion machine for
making household and birthday candles.

Eimer settled into the industry immediately and was no doubt
delighted to see the production of Christmas candles coming off the
work-benches in 1947 – the first since 1941. That Christmas the
seventy staff at the factory worked day and night to satisfy the
seasonal market, which totalled one million candles. In 1947 the
total demand for candles in Ireland was 2000 tons; before the
outbreak of war, in 1939, total candle output had been 3000 tons.
Things were looking up in the economy after the harshness of
wartime shortages and in March 1949 the company MD was
present at the reopening of the Bailey restaurant in Howth, where
the ground-floor dining room was entirely lit by candles specially
made by Rathborne's. Eimer steered the company through the
recession of the 1950s and into the exciting 1960s, when the market
for ornamental candles and birthday candles took root and opened

Left to right: *Tom Long, H.E. McCormick, Jack Entwhistle, Bill Carney, company
secretary, and Jack Daly, wax chandler, on an outing to Bray, 1951*

up new opportunities for the firm. Over the years he became an authority on the industry and its history. His enthusiasm was infectious and no doubt helped in his elevation to Honorary Secretary of the Irish Candle Makers' Association in 1949. He prepared and delivered a celebrated history of candle-making at the request of the Irish Wholesale Grocers' Association in 1949 which received national acclaim at the time.

Just after the Second World War, H.E. – called High Explosive by employees because of his zest for the job – McCormick went around Ireland with the company sales and delivery personnel and collected a wealth of oral historical material on candles. He found that the midlands attached special significance to the feast of Candlemas and that as well as the ordinary wax candle, little coloured candles were distributed after mass on 2 February. Each person was given one of these candles at the altar rails, and after kissing it they departed from the rails. Another custom which he recorded related to Longwood, County Meath, where on Candlemas the head of the household lit a candle as soon as the other members of the family returned home from mass; he then blessed himself, making a sign of the cross with the lighted candle, barely touching the flame to the lapel of his coat. All members of the family in turn blessed themselves likewise, each one touching the flame to the outer garment. The candle was then put away and lit in times of danger or stress.

With the world economy growing after the end of the Second World War, Rathborne's succeeded in securing their operations at East Wall through successful exploitation of overseas markets, which were of great importance to the firm. In the 1950s and early 1960s the African market was quite lucrative, with the firm exporting over 700 tons of candles a year to that continent. In November 1957 the company shipped twelve tons of decorative candles to Canada; in July 1961 it exported £12,000-worth of ornamental candles for use at diplomatic and trade dinner functions in the USA and in November of that year a consignment of seventy tons – nearly ten million candles – was shipped by Rathborne's to west Africa.

During the 1950s the company introduced a special Irish candle designed specifically for the US market – a gracefully tapered candle tastefully decorated with a spray of shamrock. This product became quite a vogue in Irish-American circles for St Patrick's Day throughout the 1950s. In 1961 Rathborne's patented a pearlised candle for a German firm which the company estimated could be worth up to £250,000 per annum; in the same year the company's exports totalled £100,000, up from £60,000 for the previous year. Eimer McCormick steered the company through the

H.E. McCormick presenting giant St Patrick's Day candle in U.S.A.

difficult trading conditions of the 1960s – a testing period when, coming out of the recession of the 1950s, a people no longer dependent on the candle as a source of light were only at the dawn of the new consumer society. By the end of the 1950s, that decade of unemployment and emigration, an ornamental candle market was only just beginning to take root and become established in Ireland, and this market the firm carefully nurtured. In the more competitive post-war domestic candle market it became apparent that there would have to be some rationalisation in the industry if the craft of candle-making were to survive in Ireland. In 1966 Eimer oversaw a major reorganisation in the form of the amalgamation of Lalor Candles Limited and John G. Rathborne & Company Limited, with all activities of Lalor's being transferred to East Wall. The merger made Rathborne's the country's largest supplier of church candles. Eimer remained in charge of the new heavyweight in the Irish candle manufacturing industry and continued as Managing Director until his retirement in 1974, when he was replaced by Niall Sheerin, former marketing manager of the firm.

Lalor Candles

Compared with Rathborne's, Lalor Candles was an infant company, having been founded in 1910 by A.J. Lalor, who served his time in the trade with Hayes & Finch Limited, candle manufacturers founded in Liverpool in 1880 and with a subsidiary branch in Ireland, based at 3 Eustace Street, Dublin. Lalor's first move was to secure the services of Joe Little, who was a beeswax expert with Hayes & Finch. Little had commenced his working life at Dunsinea with Rathborne's, following in the footsteps of his father and grandfather. He left Rathborne's in 1899 to take up a high-paying job as production manager with Hayes & Finch in 1899. He returned to Dublin in 1910 to take up work with Lalor. However, Little appears to have been tied to Hayes & Finch, who took a civil action against him for breach of contract. Following the litigation (the documents relating to the case were lost in the Four Courts fire during the Civil War in 1922) he had to leave Lalor, spending the rest of his working life with Hayes & Finch, retiring from that firm in 1947 after a long career in the trade. Theresa Treacher, his daughter, stated that the proceedings were bitter – 'the other side were represented by Edward Carson, who was one of the best legal personalities of the time'. Pointing to a corner of the kitchen in her Drimnagh home, she recalled that 'after the Court action all he was left with was that rocking chair over there in the corner'.

An interesting advertisement appears in the *Irish Times* in 1910, under the heading 'Altar Candles'. It reads:

> Encourage a Genuine Irish Industry. Messrs LALOR LIMITED beg to inform the Clergy and heads of Religious Communities that their Factory is now open, and they are ready to supply all orders entrusted to them for Holy Mass Candles 75% or 65% Beeswax, Vegetable Candles, Altar Candles 25% Beeswax, Shrine Candles, Night Lights, Sanctuary Oil, Wicks and Floats, Incense, Charcoal, &c., &c. Samples on Application. All Candles made under the personal supervision of A.J. Lalor, late Manager, and J. Little, Late Beeswax Expert of Hayes &

Finch Limited. Telephone 1030. LALOR LIMITED. Office: 14, Lower Ormond Quay, Dublin. Factory: Great Strand Street. P.S.— Our Candles are approved of and sanctioned by the Hierarchy and Clergy of Ireland.

One of Lalor's Directors was Cathal Brugha, a patriot and hero of the War of Independence, who had also worked with A.J. Lalor in Hayes & Finch, being that company's sales representative. It is no surprise therefore that the factory was a hotbed of intrigue during the War of Independence, and old Lalor employees have many colourful stories from that era. One relates to Michael Collins, who was said to have donned the overalls of a candle-maker and was placed on the carousel making candle dips while the Black and Tans searched the premises. When Neil Jordan's film on the life of Collins was being shot during 1995, one of the locations considered was Rathborne's factory at East Wall Road. It was proposed to shoot scenes in the old part of the factory, which houses the moulding machinery that was in use at Lalor's during Collins' lifetime. No replicas would have been required – the original machinery is still in place.

Though the premises did not, in the end, feature in the film, it has, however, featured on the cinematographer's reel, when *The Woman Who Married Clark Gable* was shot on the premises in 1985. A half-hour picture directed by Thaddeus O'Sullivan and based on the short story by Seán Ó Faoláin, the cast included Bob Hoskins, Brenda Fricker, Peter Caffrey, Eamon Kelly, Helen Roche and Eugene Kavanagh. The 'man in factory' is the master candle-maker Bobby Leppla, a familiar fixture in the factory who on 10 October 1997 celebrated fifty years of continuous work with Rathborne's. Other staff are seen in the background of the film, doing their normal work.

The film, which is set in 1930s Dublin, concerns George, a Protestant Londoner, who works in a candle factory and is married to a devout Catholic, Mary, who prays for his conversion at her bedside every night. Their life is placid enough until George decides to grow a moustache. By coincidence the couple see the film *San Francisco* and Mary becomes obsessed with the similarity between her husband and the faithless Blackie, a character played by Clark Gable, and a parallel between herself and the character of Mary, played by Jeanette MacDonald. This obsession is fuelled by a movie magazine's report about Gable having an affair. The strain on the relationship continues until George, concerned at Mary's increasingly odd behaviour, shaves off his moustache. When she sees him without it she faints, but they quickly return to domestic normality, and the film running at the picture house changes to *Bringing Up Baby*.

A great change in the company came in the early 1980s. In August 1983 the share capital was increased to £600,000 with the bulk of the shares being held by Candles Limited of Battersea, London, and a nominal three shares being held by Prices Patent Candle Company Limited, Belmont Works, London. Major investment in new machinery followed, together with a rational-isation programme that saw the numbers in employment being reduced to the present-day complement of around twenty-eight staff, covering all areas of the business from master candle-maker to sales and marketing, packing and management.

At top management level, Niall Sheerin was succeeded as managing director by Richard Tuite and he in turn was succeeded by Brian Rowan; the present incumbent is Peadar Lennon, who took over the helm in 1989. It is interesting to note that Peadar is just the sixth managing director at the company to come from outside the Rathborne family. In his previous position as the Marine & Aviation Manager of Irish Shell, part of Peadar's brief was selling lubricants for jet engines, so there was a huge shift from tech-nological sales expertise to the humble world of the ordinary household candle. A native of Cootehill, Co. Cavan, he oversaw the development of the factory shop while refurbishing the façade, and steered the company into a period of steady growth in production and sales. He sees a bright future for Rathborne's:

> The market at home and abroad will continue to thrive. On the personal use side, in Ireland we are only burning a fraction of what continental Europeans burn, so there is tremendous potential for us in this sector of the market. I

see continuing developments in the styling and range of domestic candles – already we stock hundreds of styles, colours and sizes of candle to suit every taste imaginable. Over the past few years there has been a substantial increase in our exports of church candles to the UK.

Following in the footsteps of John G. and other members of the Rathborne family, Peadar has seen the firm taking part in a number of trade fairs at home and abroad. Their participation in the 1997 Top Drawer Fair in London, whose organisers are most selective in choosing their exhibitors, resulted in lucrative orders in the non-church candle market in the UK. Taking part in this prestigious event proved a resounding success for the firm, so much so that a Saudi customer purchased the entire stock on display at the close of the fair. Their participation in the same event in 1998 was equally successful, with huge overseas interest in the company's varied, innovative and colourful products.

When talking about the shop in the factory, which is open to the public during normal working hours, Peadar draws attention to the fact that it is a great testing ground for the company's market. Situated on the East Wall Road, on the main route to the East Link Bridge, the shop attracts increasing numbers of tourists and commuters, as well as the occasional school or group tours. With a huge stock on display, the fastest-selling lines are an indication to the company of where to place the emphasis in production and marketing.

Quality Control

One of the key areas in any manufacturing concern today is quality control, and this is where Rathborne's have always maintained the highest standards down through the years. The experience of Peg Buckley (now Peg Ladrigan) of Carnlough Road, who moved to Cabra West with her mother Elizabeth and family in 1941 following the bombing of the North Strand, is typical. Peg recalls:

When I married we moved into the family home. I remember the summer of 1965, Mammy bought a few boxes of night lights in Londis Supermarket for her Sacred Heart altar. After a few days she said that there was something wrong with the candles, that they were burning out too fast. She wrote to Rathborne's about it. They sent out a man and he took the candles away to test them. He called back a few weeks later and said that the supply of imported wax which went into her night lights had a small quantity of sand in it. This affected the burning and that is why they burnt out so quickly. He said that they had recalled the full batch from the shops. A week after that she had a lovely letter from Rathborne's along with a few boxes of night lights. She kept the letter with all her trinkets.

Candle Production

Candle manufacturing today is a year-round process, punctuated by periods of very heavy demand such as Christmas, Candlemas (in February) and Easter. At Rathborne's the most modern machinery now turns out millions of candles every year, though thousands of beeswax candles are still hand-crafted by the firm's master chandlers using age-old techniques of repeatedly pouring molten wax over wicks hanging from iron hoops. The busiest time of the year for the candle-maker is still Christmas time. Although the purchase of candles for display in the windows of ordinary domestic houses – an old Irish tradition – has diminished since the 1960s, candles are bought in huge numbers as gifts or for use on the table for adding to the atmosphere of seasonal mealtimes.

Candlemas Day

Demand for candles for Candlemas Day is so high that as soon as the Christmas market is satisfied, production at Rathborne's is again at peak output, with staff again working overtime in order to meet the market needs for this occasion. Candlemas Day, celebrated on 2 February, commemorates the visit of the Virgin Mary to the temple forty days after the birth of Jesus, in order to be purified according to the strict Jewish laws of the time and also to present the infant Jesus to God as her first-born (Luke 2:22-38). Formerly called 'The Purification of the Blessed Virgin Mary', it is now celebrated by the Roman Catholic Church as 'The Presentation of our Lord'. Sometime during the early fifth century AD the practice of observing this festival with lighted candles had been introduced and the name Candlemas developed from this new tradition. The earliest reference to the festival is from Jerusalem, where in the fourth century AD the western pilgrim Etheria attended that town's celebrations on 14 February, which was forty days after the feast of the Epiphany. She wrote about the occasion in the *Peregrinatio Etheriae*. The celebration of the festival spread far and wide and in 542 AD the Emperor Justinian I decreed that its date should be moved back to 2 February, forty days after Christmas.

Candlemas Day has been celebrated in Ireland for centuries and with it were associated some of our most delightful traditions. One historical document relates that in the year 1500 the Chapel of the Hospital of Crutched Friars of St John the Baptist at Kells, County Cavan, was illuminated by five hundred candles at Candlemas. Another record relates that following Oliver Cromwell's murderous sacking of Drogheda in 1649, many people who had gathered in a barn to celebrate the feast of Candlemas the following year were taken out and put to death. A Candlemas gift appears in the will of Allart Clasen Vanwycke of Dundalk, who in 1639 bequeathed an endowment of five pounds to the town to buy 'Mary gallons for the poor inhabitants' on that day. 'Mary gallons' refers to ale or spirit given in honour of the Blessed Virgin Mary. In the middle ages it was the custom in some parts of Ireland to give donations to teachers and instructors in arts and crafts on Candlemas Day. There are some records in existence to prove that the masters of the hedge-schools received money from parents on this day.

Candles – A Part of Life

Strange as it may seem, in this age of nuclear fuel and alternative energy sources, the candle still has a place in modern-day living.

Though carving a market share is no easy task in today's world, Rathborne's has managed to not only maintain market share for their 3000-year-old product but is actually prospering with it.

'I am taking part in a survey of what business will be like in the year 2020, and I can say with certainty that the candle will be with us then.' So says one of the leading entrepreneurs on the Irish business scene, Feargal Quinn, who heads the Superquinn chain of supermarkets. He was fascinated to find that something like a candle could have a place in our everyday lives. He saw that a gap had appeared in the market for the ornamental candle, and so he placed an order with Rathborne's for handmade, hand-wrapped beeswax candles. Conscious that there is a future for tradition and that people are anxious to retain links with the past, he was certain that the venture would meet with success. 'Of course, it was a new departure for us and it was our first ever order for handmade beeswax candles.'

A handmade product will be more expensive by definition than a mass-produced product, but Feargal feels that in this particular area price is secondary; it is quality and craftsmanship that really counts:

> If it is just light that you want, the mass-produced candle will do the job; but if you are looking for atmosphere, the shape, colour and design of the candle are important as is the ability of the candle supplier to tie in with place settings; it is important for the candle and napkin manu-facturer to operate in a co-operative, complementary manner.

There are many candle buffs around and Feargal Quinn's wife Denise is an avid enthusiast: 'I brought her home two candles from South Africa in the shape of ostrich eggs and she loved them. We eat outdoors a lot, very often by candlelight. Denise also believes that candles keep flies away from the outdoor meal table.'

Although a staunch supporter of Irish-made goods, Feargal is the first to say that there is no room for sentiment in the market-place. Superquinn promotes Irish goods by displaying a shamrock in front of the product, but 'we went a step further by adapting technology to identify on the receipt the Irish-made products and also the percentage of the customers' bill that is made up of Irish-manufactured goods. This, we believe, has enabled the customer to compare the Irish product to the imported one and is also a reminder to them of the fact that the product listed on their receipt is a native one.' Modern technology has, he feels, helped Irish manufacturing and he hopes that it will lead to the Irish-made candle increasing its market share.

Another big player on the Irish retail scene is Tesco Ireland, which took over the giant Quinnsworth/Crazy Prices group in 1997. Their marketing guru is Maurice Pratt, who enthuses about Rathborne's products:

> It is great to see an old firm like Rathborne's moving so powerfully into the next millennium. We have been retailing their products for as long as I have been in the business. For years we only stocked candles at Christmas time, but for the past eighteen months we have stocked them on a year-round basis. We sell them countrywide and Rathborne's supply us with a first-class product. The quality of their service is excellent and they offer a wide variety of candles, with in-stock positions and a changing choice due to having a deft finger on fashions.
>
> Candles have long surpassed their functions of yesteryear, when they were just red or white and were purchased for either Christmas or for the dinner table. I also remember the time when they were burned so as to reduce the volume of cigarette smoke in a room, though I don't know if that was an old wives' tale. Candles really took off with the development of floating candles and with their use as a mood-setter. They are now a treat purchase and are remarkably fashionable. I can see a growing and lucrative market for candles – and Rathborne's – with the development of apartment living not only in Dublin but throughout Ireland. With smaller domestic unit sizes there is a growing trend to use candles not only for atmosphere but as an alternative to electric light.

Rathborne's supplies other major players on the Irish retail scene, including Supervalu, Centra, Spar and Musgraves. Looking after these orders and the individual needs of clients is Terry Roche. Originally from Dublin's Pimlico area and now living in Rathfarnham, Terry started off his working life in Lalor Candles on 1 September 1957 and has spent all his career in candle sales. He remembers his own father, who for many years ran a shop in Pimlico called The Bungalow, giving out candles every Christmas to his regular customers, 'the ones whose messages go down in the book, and of course the candles were red Rathborne's, purchased from O. & R. Fry, Wholesalers of Hawkins Street'. The biggest market for the company is the Irish one but from time to time export markets are satisfied: 'at present we are filling a UK order for votive lights'. Such is the demand for ornamental and votive candles that the company is flat-out just satisfying the home demand, which makes Terry a very busy man. He has an all-round knowledge of his product: 'Candles are also made from vegetable oils – did you know that the British Army gave edible candles, made in London, to their troops as they embarked for the Falklands War?'. In true Rathborne

Terry Roche at a 1960s trade fair showing off Rathborne's products

fashion, another generation of the Roche family has entered the business and Terry's son Carl now works with the firm.

The candle is also a necessary item for the modern-day adventurer and explorer; for example the well-known Irish climber Frank Nugent, who took part in the successful Irish conquest of Mount Everest in 1993 and in the South Arís adventure in the Antarctic in 1997 (which commemorated Kildare-born Ernest Shackleton's epic voyage and brave attempt to cross Antarctica from the Weddell Sea to the Ross Sea in 1914–16), always takes a supply of candles with him for emergencies.

The market for beeswax candles is still church-dominated and provides steady business for the company on a year-round basis. An example of the importance of this particular market sector for the candle industry comes from the parish of Cabra West, where during a week-long Mission in April 1996 approximately five thousand candles were lit in the Church of the Most Precious Blood. It was the first Mission in the parish in more than twenty years but its success and the volume of candle sales in the church shop astounded the parish priest, Fr Cecil Johnston. In addition to the steady church market there is now an ever-growing demand in the restaurant, pub and domestic sectors of the candle market.

The percentage of pure beeswax used is now down to an average of 25 per cent and this is due to historical factors. The price of beeswax in 1910 was between £140 and £150 a ton. In the 1960s the cost had increased considerably, to £700 a ton compared with £70 per ton for paraffin wax. In the early 1970s the world experienced an acute shortage of beeswax due, says Terry Roche, 'to the introduction of the African bee to South America, a major world supplier of the product. This resulted in the decimation of the native bee population and as a result local churches sought the approval of the Vatican to reduce the content of beeswax in candles used for religious purposes from the then standard 65 to 51 per cent. Over the years the quantity of beeswax continued to be reduced, mainly as a result of the high cost of the product, until it reached the present-day standard of 25 per cent pure beeswax.'

Bobby Leppla adds his own fifty years of experience to the already centuries-old traditional method of hand-casting wax candle at the Dublin factory. Bobby's grandfather was a straw hatmaker in the Dublin Liberties, while he started making his first candles at the age of thirteen

Candlelight – Some People Remember

There are countless people who can still remember the times when the candle was a major source of light in their own home. Indeed, when one considers that the Black Valley in County Kerry was only connected to the National Grid in the 1970s, it is not surprising that there are some relatively young people around who remember going to bed by candlelight. Tim Doyle, author of *Peaks and Valleys*, a book on the ups and downs of a young Garda, grew up in mid-Kerry and was in his late teens when electricity came to his home during the 1960s: 'I think I was a Garda before we got electricity in our home. I always did my homework by candlelight and one of my abiding memories is going to sleep with the smell of candles in my nostrils.'

The rush-lights were the first candles that Tommy Kenny from Ballinasloe remembers. Later, as living conditions improved in the 1930s, he recalls buying candles in the local shop every week, at a cost of just one penny each. The candles were held steady 'in an iron thing with a yoke up near the top of it that you put the candle in and you could turn it any way you wanted. It was very thin and about a foot high; the local blacksmiths made these holders.'

Tommy also recalls lantern candles, which were hung outside houses and on the side of a horse-drawn carriage. Kathleen Connolly from Lecklevera, who is mentioned in a previous chapter, only got electricity in the mid-1960s. She recalls using candles as a supplement to the oil lamps: 'We had two oil lamps, a table lamp in the parlour and a wall lamp in the kitchen, over the fireplace. We used candles in the bedroom and downstairs as extra light for the children doing their exercise. During the Economic War in the early 1930s when oil was scarce and rationed, we used candles as the main source of light. I didn't get the electricity until the 1960s. I used to buy candles by the dozen and by the half-dozen. I only got white candles and they were always Rathborne candles.'

Denis Long, from Inniscarragh, County Cork, was born in 1907 and was sixteen years old before he saw electric light, when he went to live with an aunt in Macroom. He recalled this time: 'I was reared by candlelight. I always remember the Christmas candle, which was a fairly big one. The ordinary ones were bought when my parents went to Cork for groceries. The candles came in a paper packet of twelve and were about nine inches long. We put them in a metal dish when burning them.' Rosaleen Boyne from Poppintree in Dublin recalls her early years in Eccles Street, where the only light in the bedrooms was from the candle. She remembers the night of the North Strand bombing in 1941, when all the children in the tenement house she lived in were brought by candlelight into a large drawing room on the ground floor, where all the candles were snuffed out and they spent the night in darkness. 'Sometimes we had to borrow a penny to buy a candle. The candles were all from Rathborne's and we used the kitchen fat to hold the candle steady on the table.'

Electric light did not arrive in the home of Kathleen McDarby, from Carlow town, until the early 1930s: 'Up until then we had paraffin oil lamps downstairs and candles upstairs. When you went to bed, you'd always have a candle to take up with you. I remember reading in bed with a candle. My mother would shout up to me telling me not to set the house on fire.' Paddy O'Sullivan, from Adraville, Scartaglen, grew up on a farm: 'The farm had forty cows and two horses. My family did not get electricity until 1948 and by that time I had left home and settled in Dublin. We had paraffin oil lamps and whenever you ran out of oil, we used candles. The lighted candle was put in a sconce. This was round like a saucer, with a hole in it for the candle. The sconce was made from enamel or tin. We went to bed by candlelight.'

Bernadette Brady (née Curley) from Killykespin, near Smithboro in County Monaghan, recalls going to bed by candlelight: 'We had a tilly lamp in the kitchen and when bedtime came my mother got the sconce, made of pottery, which had a little holder on it, lit the candle and brought us to bed. The candle remained lit in the bedroom until we all went asleep. The candles came from Rathborne's in Dublin and were of the size of twelve to the pound. We bought several packets at a time and they came wrapped by the dozen in brown paper. I remember the packets were first sealed with glue. We burned candles until electricity came to the area in April 1960. After that, while there was always candles in the house for emergencies, we only bought them in twos or threes.'

'I remember all my brothers and sisters and myself trying to do our exercise by the light of one candle,' recalls Rose O'Driscoll, from Tipperkevin, County Kildare. 'Someone would shout, "The shadow of your head is on my copy", and the candle would have to be raised. Even in the bedroom there was a candle, and if you died you were waked by three candles. They had to be wax candles and someone would be sent to Naas to buy them. The candles were placed on a table beside the corpse and there would be some hedge on the table, which would be dipped in the Holy Water by visitors, who then sprinkled the corpse. You always had to have a good supply of candles in the house as the nearest shop was nearly four miles away.' Rose got married and moved to Cabra West during the Emergency: 'This was the time of the shortages. There were only two lights in the house, one on the landing and one in the kitchen, as there was a shortage of electric cable to wire the whole house, so we used candles until the end of the shortages. We burned Rathborne candles, which cost a penny each in the Fassaugh Stores.'

East Wall district, 1912. Arrow shows location of Rathborne's (Dublin Petroleum Stores)

Dispatch area, East Wall, 1928

Works yard, East Wall, 1928. Note wooden barrel for wax transportation

CHAPTER FIVE

Advertising & Marketing

In the days before radio and television and the advent of modern marketing, the major promotional events in the world of business and industry were trade fairs and exhibitions. The earliest evidence of Rathborne participation in such events was the Irish Industrial Exhibition of 1853, which took place on Leinster Lawn, Kildare Street, Dublin. The Rathborne products on display included 'crude oil from the spermaceti whale and a block of refined spermaceti, illustrative of its crystallization'. A pyramid of crystallised spermaceti was one of the items displayed in the central hall, and 'beeswax candles were also on show with their various degrees of manufacture illustrated'. At the Dublin International Exhibition of 1865, which was held in Earlsfort Terrace, 'John G. Rathborne of Essex Street showed unbleached and bleached beeswax; candles and sperm oil; spermaceti crude and refined; sealing wax etc.' The firm was awarded a medal, presented to the proud John G., for the superior quality of the wax and sperm candles on display. An interesting anecdote is thrown up on this occasion, for after John G. received the award, he received another one from his own staff upon his return to the factory that same evening – an illuminated address presented to him by his workers to mark the occasion of his marriage to Eliza Burnley. The testimonial still survives and is displayed in a glass frame in the company's boardroom at East Wall.

Every industrial trade event in the calendar was supported by Rathborne's. John G.'s son, Henry Burnley, was a great supporter of Irish industry and endeavour and played a significant role in the Irish International Exhibition of 1907 at Herbert Park. This Exhibition was unique for the firm, for not only did it have exhibits of beeswax, spermaceti, stearine and paraffin candles but also its 'ideal bicycle lighting apparatus', a candle bicycle-lamp – a form of lighting much preferred by lady cyclists at this time due to its cleanliness. Henry B. manned the company's stand himself all during the Exhibition, and enthused about the 'reliability and efficient nature' of the company's bicycle candle. He no doubt also chatted to business people and the public about the special qualities of a Rathborne candle.

The firm spent most of its direct promotional budget running advertisements in religious publications, with occasional advertising in daily newspapers like the *Irish Times*, and this was a feature of its marketing all during the early and mid-1900s. They also advertised in the promotional catalogues of big department stores like Healy's of Dame Street and Pim's of Mary Street. A considerable amount of Rathborne's promotional efforts were concentrated on the whole-sale end of the market. The company fostered goodwill and strong links with the wholesale trade, and the office regularly wrote directly to wholesalers and church clients promoting their product and keeping them notified of any price variations.

During Eimer McCormick's time as Managing Director from 1946 to 1974 the company opened up new and lucrative markets in the USA. The market was established when, in 1949, a request from Boston for church candles was diverted to the firm by an Irish businessman who had been visiting that city. With a toehold in the US market from this request, Eimer built up a lucrative trade for Rathborne's. His advertising ploy was by way of business contacts and through getting press coverage in the ordinary news columns of local newspapers throughout the eastern states of the USA. He also established and developed strong trading links with a number of North American oil companies and in this way the firm carved out an important market niche. Eimer went on annual promotional trips to the USA for over thirty years and these tours secured plenty of media coverage for the company. On the home front he gave talks, lectures and interviews on customs relating to candles, and on the history of both candles and Rathborne's. He recalls doing a radio interview for Radio Éireann with Terry O'Sullivan, a well-known *Evening Press* journalist, on the tradition and history of the candle.

One of the early marketing tools which the company used during this time was the presentation of six- to eight-foot-long decorated candles for occasions such as the centenary of a town or the silver or golden jubilee of a large company or the birthday of the head of an important Rathborne customer. On one occasion Eimer personally presented an eight-foot-high candle to the mother of an oil company head to mark her 90th birthday. The event was covered throughout the USA by the media, ensuring a high profile for Rathborne's. In 1957 a six-foot candle was presented to the city of Montreal for the St Patrick's Day festivities and in 1958 the company earned huge newspaper coverage throughout Europe when it made its biggest candle ever, a fifteen-foot high 500-pound wax candle, fourteen inches in diameter, which burned over the twelve days of Christmas at London Airport. It was presented as a gift to the people of England by Aer Lingus and the Irish Export Centre. In 1972 British Airways flew an eight-foot candle, ten inches in diameter and weighing 144 pounds, to Melbourne for the Australian International Gift Fair.

H.E. McCormick, Rathborne's, and Helen Bourke, BEA hostess, with giant candle for the Australian International Gift Fair, Melbourne, 1970

Down through the years the media have shown a remarkable interest in the art of candle-making. Even today, many people will remark about how much they enjoyed the *Hands* documentary, which appeared on RTÉ in 1980, whenever the name of Rathborne's is mentioned. Writer and historian Éamonn Mac Thomáis researched and narrated the documentary and thoroughly enjoyed the task: 'I have always had an interest in candles; I think it is in the genes, for some years ago, while looking up the family tree, I discovered that my ancestors were candle-makers and I came across a James Thomas, chandler and soap-boiler of Redmond Hill. My father's name was also James Thomas.' Éamonn 'grew up with candles. My father died when I was young and the bills were harder to meet. The electric meter took a shilling, and to make that last the week, we also used oil lamps and candles. I did my eccer by candlelight, went to bed by candlelight, read comics by candlelight. And do you know I once met a man called Lightholder?'

The installation of electric votive lights in some churches has disappointed many people, including Éamonn. 'A candle flickering shows hope. If this trend continues we will be renouncing the devil with flashlamps.' Like many people, Éamonn does not feel that electric votive lamps can compare with candles: 'I don't know how many times I put in my money and pressed the button and nothing happened. I pressed more buttons and still did not get a light. You can't beat a candle. They will always be with us because when the lights go out there will always be a candle around.'

Though Rathborne's has long enjoyed brand recognition it is only in the past few years that the firm's corporate image has gained a recognisable national profile. Colin O'Carroll was Marketing Manager of Rathborne's for three years and during his tenure the firm became more widely identified in Irish life. Speaking in 1992 he said that he felt there was no need to re-launch the product:

> Older people knew the brand well enough already. The company's products were excellent and the quality unrivalled. However, due to a traditional market, incorporating the purchase of candles for church use and for Christmas time, the profile of the firm and name of

Rathborne's remained in the background. In the new, highly developing non-traditional market sector, which looked to candles for ambience and atmosphere, the company brand was not at all that well known with what was by and large a younger market.

The effort put into marketing and presentation by the company since the early 1990s has paid off and many more Dubliners now know where Rathborne's is located, 'which was not common knowledge a few years ago', recalls Colin. The candle factory has enjoyed great support since, with group and school tours a regular occurrence and countless numbers of individual callers, both visitors from around the country and tourists from around the world. On one particular day over eight different nationalities visited the shop and factory.

During 1995 Rathborne's featured in the RTÉ *Live at Three* programme which was devoted to candle-making, and again the subject proved a most popular one with the TV audience. In April 1995 Rathborne's also featured in the Australian Channel 9 TV programme *Today* during a special two-hour feature on Ireland. While holidaying in Queensland during August 1996 the author heard local people talking about 'the five-hundred year-old candle factory in Dublin'. Colin left Rathborne's for other career horizons within the Shell group in November 1995, but still nurtures a deep love for the firm.

Colin O'Carroll was succeeded in the post of Marketing Manager by Justin Kneeshaw, who has the task of satisfying and responding to an ever-changing and increasingly sophisticated ornamental candle market and steering the company into the sophisticated markets of the new millennium. He has seen a remarkable growth in the ornamental and general retail sector of the candle trade and sees a bright future for the company. He feels that more people than ever before know Rathborne's. His brother Andrew also works at Rathborne's, where he manages the shop. 'I have been here two years and the shop has really taken off in that time. What many people don't know is that we can supply any customer with whatever they want, no matter how small their order is. For example, we will

*Advertisement in 'Irish Hotelier',
March 1950*

engrave wax candles with individual messages for any special occasion, be it a wedding or a christening. We also hope to open a Visitor Centre here on East Wall Road, sometime during the year 2000.' It is interesting to note that descendants of the Kneeshaws, who came over to Ireland from Maltan, Yorkshire, also established themselves in the illumination industry, establishing a gas company in Clonmel, County Tipperary. Assisting Justin is the firm's Business Development Manager, David Buggy, who looks after the requirements of hotel, restaurant and gift-shop clients and the general retail segment of the market. One of his concepts is a beautiful wooden box containing a half-dozen six-inch wax candles, tied with a ribbon and with a section for a box of matches. The outside of the box has the crest of the Tallow Chandlers Guild and can be hung on a wall in the kitchen or hall of the home.

Everlasting Candlelight

It appears that we still enjoy a deep love of candles, a love probably born of past generations of dependence on them as a source of light. The main use of candles in the western world is for ornamental and atmosphere-enhancing use; many films have featured candles in the background, and *As Good as It Gets, Barry Lyndon, The Boxer, The Butcher Boy, Devil's Advocate, Reality Bites, The Spy Who Came In from the Cold* and *The Towering Inferno* are just some examples of the many recent and not-so-recent films to hit our picture-house screens featuring burning candles. Indeed in *The Spy Who Came In from the Cold*, shot on location in Smithfield, Dublin 7, just a stone's throw away from where the Rathborne Prussia Street factory operated, the humble candle features prominently in the candlelight suppers of assistant-librarian Nan Perry (played by Claire Bloom), when she entertains the spy Alex Lemas (played by Richard Burton) in her home. Rathborne's supplied the candles for *Barry Lyndon*, *The Boxer* and *The Butcher Boy*, and they also supplied the candles which appear in scenes for the hugely popular TV drama *Ballykissangel*, set in County Wicklow.

Of course our need for candlelight is always 'just around the corner' – in the event of a power cut the first thing people look for is a candle. To the developed world, the war in Bosnia showed, in an unfortunate sense, our continuing dependence on the candle not only as a source of light but as a source of heat as well. With the breakdown of public services as a result of the war, a great proportion of the Bosnian population became dependant on the candle for both light and heat. In February 1994 Rathborne's provided twelve tons of Amnesty International candles for Bosnia, arranging two transports from an American Air Force base in Germany to fly in the candles for mass civilian use. Each candle carried the Amnesty logo and the simple message 'Candles are both Light and Heat'.

H.E. McCormick with office staff, 1951.
Back row: *Mr Cleave, Niall Sheerin, Tom Long, Jack Entwhistle, Christy Moran*
Front row: *E. Fuller, W. Carney, Ms Whyte, H.E. McCormick, Ms Stacey,*
Mr Reilly

Reception hatch and office, East Wall, 1928

Chapter Six

The Workers' Perspective

In the course of researching the history of John G. Rathborne & Co. Ltd, I interviewed many present and former employees of the firm, and each one had strings of happy memories and anecdotes. The common theme was a tremendous sense of camaraderie between all employees, from the highest rank down to the gatekeeper. Éamonn Mac Thomáis puts this unique work ethic and lifestyle down to the close relationship between the production of a candle and the need to sell it:

> I felt that the good atmosphere came from everyone being
> so conscious of the fact that 'if we don't get orders we will
> not be here'. The joy in the work emanates from Bobby
> Leppla, who takes great pride in his handicraft and work,
> a pride that extends to everybody in the factory, from top
> to bottom.

Certainly there is tremendous admiration and respect within the factory for the craft worker, the producer of the handmade candle, and this is felt in all areas at the firm. But there is tremendous respect within the company for the worth and contribution of each individual across all divisions of work, from production to sales and delivery. It would appear that Rathborne's has had, from an early time, the corporate 'white stone' mentioned by Charles Handy in his book entitled *The Hungry Spirit*. Handy states that if a business is, in its essentials, a collection of people, it will make more sense to think of it as a town or a village rather than a piece of property or machinery. This has always been the essence of Rathborne's, and when visitors enter the grounds of the factory they are immediately struck by the sense of community which pervades the workplace atmosphere.

For the early workers the move to the North Wall in 1925 was quite a big upheaval but every one of the employees stuck with the firm. With no public transport from areas such as Blanchardstown village, going to work became more difficult for people like Michael Stewart. Michael started work as a fourteen-year-old at Dunsinea in May 1911 and was also employed on the Rathborne farm when candle production was slack. He had to cycle to work every day from Blanchardstown after the company relocated to East Wall, only giving up the bicycle after the first public bus service commenced running through the village – the No. 70 Dunboyne bus. He used the bus to travel to East Wall for the remaining years of his working life. His daughter Monica, who works in Rathborne's, recalls his expertise: 'He was a beeswax expert and he used to make a certain candle with three candles coming from a single wax base or handle. During the war his expertise was sought by an English firm, Francis Tucker & Company. He took up the offer in December 1942 and went to London, where he was fully engaged in the crafting of handmade beeswax candles. He returned to Ireland and Rathborne's after the war, declining a lucrative offer to stay on at Tucker's.'

Around this time Michael worked under the approving eye of Jack Riley, works manager, and his co-workers included John Daly, who worked on the machine candles, George Tinkle, a Czech-born engineer, Terry Monaghan, who rolled and tipped church candles, Larry Ryan, who worked the moulding machine making household candles, and Carmel O'Reilly, Betty Meade and Betty Woods, who worked in the packing department and between them packed 8000 candles a day. The first of many company works outings began in the late 1940s and there were also outings to celebrate an employee's special day.

When Michael Stewart was marking fifty years' employment with the firm in 1961 it coincided with a gift from the directors of the company to the staff: an outing to the Holmpatrick Hotel in Skerries for 'a day's fun and games that ended at midnight with a dance', recalls a former colleague. 'It was a great day out for us all. They presented him with a colour TV and a wallet of notes.' The *Dublin Evening Mail* was there to cover the event and photographed Michael with the company's newest recruit, fourteen-year-old Kathleen Dunne from Ballyfermot. Three years later when he retired, Michael was presented with a watch and wallet. Celebrating retirement on that same day was William 'Billy' Lindsay, who worked for the construction firm which built the candle factory at East Wall Road. When Rathborne's moved into the new factory in 1925 Billy joined the firm, at twenty-eight years of age, and over the years worked in all the areas of operation.

Michael Connor was another employee who spent fifty years working with the firm, and when he retired from Rathborne's in November 1955 he brought to a close a family service record with the firm of 165 years; his father, Michael, and grandfather, also called Michael, had both joined the firm as young boys of fourteen years of age. Indeed, when a journalist with the *Times Pictorial* visited the factory in 1948 Michael was introduced to him as 'young Mick' – at 64 years of age! His father was called 'old Mick' but his grandfather was just called 'Mick'. Michael worked for over fifty years making candles before changing jobs and becoming the factory watchman towards the end of his career with the firm.

This loyalty in the candle-manufacturing industry is not unique to Rathborne's, for in the mid-1950s the Mayor of Battersea, London, Councillor Lang, at the opening of the redeveloped Price's Patent Candles factory there, met six male employees with a combined total of 303 years' service and three female employees with a combined total service of 135 years, who were chosen out of a staff of three hundred people.

The Horan family from Blackhorse Lane (now Blackhorse Avenue) is one of the many families there that was for generations associated with Rathborne's. Peggy Horan started work with Rathborne's in 1948 and worked with Carmel O'Reilly in the candle-wrapping section and was later sent on a First Aid course and put in charge of the factory surgery, filling in the spare time with office work. She used to cycle to work from Blackhorse Avenue, where she still lives. She left the firm in 1955 upon her marriage to Paddy Flanagan. Peggy was very happy at East Wall and recalls her time there:

> Eimer McCormick was the Managing Director and there was great excitement in the factory when they had their first baby. Mr Kearney worked in the office and Jack Reilly was the foreman. Terry Monaghan was great fun to work with and he used to cycle in to the factory from Corduff Cross, out past Blanchardstown, travelling down the Navan Road, though they all called it the High Road. Charlie English was one of the long-serving employees and Mick Stewart was the master wax-chandler and a real nice man. Maureen Barrett was the forewoman and was a very nice person to work with.
>
> My father and his family before him worked in Rathborne's. My father, Terence Horan, started work in Dunsinea and cycled there from our home at Ashtown Villas, Blackhorse Avenue. When the factory moved to East Wall, he continued cycling to work. He used to put brown paper inside his coat to keep out the biting east wind. Bill Coates was the foreman in those days. My uncle Willy Horan also worked in the factory, from 1930 to 1939. During the First World War, British Army recruiting officers visited the factory at Dunsinea and my father volunteered for service, on the guarantee that his job would be waiting for him on his return from the war. He did get his job back and worked in Rathborne's until he retired. My uncle Willie was also in the British Army. When my father died in 1953 he was buried in the Military Cemetery on Blackhorse Avenue, and uncle Willie is also buried there. Quite a few of the men on the lane joined the British Army at that time.

Peggy's father Terence is found on the Wages List for 6 January 1926, earning fifty-four shillings per week. Her brother Michael, who lives in Finglas and spent his career in An Post, served on the last Dublin-Cork mail train before the final curtain came down on that aspect of postal and rail history. Besides Peggy's father Terence, among the dead servicemen buried in the Military Cemetery on Blackhorse Avenue is Lieutenant Commander George Richard Colin Campbell of the Royal Navy, who with his wife Eileen Hester Louisa and only child Eileen Elizabeth Augusta, perished on board the RMS *Leinster*, the Dublin Steampacket Company passenger vessel, when it was torpedoed by a German U-boat in the Irish Sea just off Dun Laoghaire, on 10 October 1918, a few weeks before the end of the First World War. Nearly six hundred lives were lost in the tragedy.

Besides Peggy Horan, there are other former Rathborne families living on Blackhorse Avenue. These are the descendants of the Dalys, Dodds, Reids and McGregors, some of whom reside in the same houses their fathers or uncles lived in during the last days of the Rathborne family dynasty at Dunsinea, just before the First World War. Marjorie Daly recalls the stories of her grandfathers, Larry Daly and John Little: 'Grandfather Larry Daly used to walk to work every morning, and when the firm moved to East Wall, he continued to walk to work. He used to call in to the other workers on the lane to wake them up as he walked towards town. My aunt, Annie Dodd, who died in April 1998 at the age of ninety-one, also worked in Rathborne's.' Next door to Marjorie lives John Reid, whose father Matthew can be found on the 1923 wages list at Appendix VI. He himself went to East Wall when he came of working age, and was interviewed by Mr Sloan:

> I remember it well. Bill Coates, the gate man, gave me the rundown before I was interviewed and was very kind to me. I got the job but never took it up as something local came my way and I didn't fancy the long journey to the candle factory. My father started his working life in Dunsinea and used to walk to work every day. When the firm moved to East Wall he used to walk to Conyngham

John Reid outside his home on Blackhorse Avenue. His family and neighbouring families left these cottages every morning to work in Rathborne's, Dunsinea.
(PHOTO BERNARD NEARY)

Road, going through the Phoenix Park at the hole-in-the-wall, and he caught the tram to Ballybough Bridge, from where he walked down to the factory. He later got a bike and cycled to work every day. He never missed a single day during all his years at work. Larry Daly next door used to call him as he walked down the lane for work. He was a great walker and believe it or not he used walk all the way into East Wall.

Theresa Treacher lived in Drimnagh for most of her life and when interviewed in her home she cheerily admitted to being 'ninety-four years young'; she never worked in Rathborne's and made her living touching up pictures in Lafayette's, where the present-day offices of the *Irish Times* are situated in D'Olier Street. 'I touched up pictures of de Valera and Catherine McAuley,' she fondly recalled. She began her working life in Lafayette's factory, which was then situated beside the Basin at Blessington Street, on Dublin's north side, and married the manager's son, Herbert Treacher. What has Theresa got to do with Rathborne's? Her maiden name was Little and she 'grew up on Blackhorse Lane. It's now got posh and is called Blackhorse Avenue. My father, grandfather and great-grandfather all worked in Rathborne's at Dunsinea.' Her father, Joe Little, was a beeswax expert and followed family tradition by joining his own father, John Little, at Rathborne's in 1874. He left Rathborne's in 1901 to take a job in Liverpool with the English candle-makers Hayes & Finch. Theresa was born in Liverpool that year and grew up

Theresa Treacher (née Little), 1995
(PHOTO BERNARD NEARY)

with candles – she remembered the bleaching fields where the wax was naturally dyed by the sun, which she first saw as a toddler. Joe Little came back to Ireland in 1910 to work with the new candle-making firm of Lalor's, and a newspaper advertisement in the *Irish Times* from that period described him as a 'beeswax expert, late of Hayes & Finch'. Shortly after that Joe, following bitter litigation, went back to Hayes & Finch at Eustace Street, where he saw out his working life. He died in 1944 at the age of eighty-seven. Theresa enthused about the famous candle-manufacturing company:

> Rathborne's and the Little family were, like many other families in the Blackhorse Lane and Ashtown district, closely linked, and my auntie Kate Little was married to Paddy Duff, who also worked at Dunsinea. Ned Daly, who also worked at Rathborne's, married my first cousin, Rita Dodd. A number of the Dodds worked there too. My grandfather, John Little, retired from Rathborne's the year I was born. Rathborne's used to be near Little Brittain Street and my mother's sister Mary worked in that street – she was housekeeper to Barney Kernan, the

racehorse trainer. My family also was interested in sport
and my brother Joe Little was a founder of the famous
Home Farm soccer club; he died in 1974.

Our home was filled with stories about Rathborne's and
I remember my father telling us that in 1820 there were
no less than thirteen Littles, from five different families,
working in Dunsinea and that on one occasion in the
1870s there were three generations of his own family
employed at the plant. He told me about the terrible fire
at the factory in 1895 and about the kindness of John G.
Rathborne and about his home being entirely lit by
candle, in an age when the gentry used gaslight.

The once-quiet village of Blanchardstown, now a teeming
suburb, was another area from which Rathborne's drew its labour
pool during the years at Dunsinea. Monica Stewart hails from there
and has spent the past thirty-eight years working at East Wall Road.
A charge-hand at the company, Monica did not think that she would
be that long with the firm: 'On my first day, I thought I wouldn't
stick it a month.' Monica is involved in packing and operating some
of the machines. Packing is still carried out in the old way: 'I am
presently hand-wrapping individual sizes of beeswax candles, which
are part of a special Superquinn order.' In true company tradition,
Monica is not the only member of her family to work at the trade –
her father Michael Stewart, mentioned at the start of this chapter,
spent fifty-three years with the company.

Working with Monica is fellow charge-hand Betty Byrne,
originally from Pearse Street but now living in East Wall. Betty has
been with the company for thirty years: 'Anyone that comes in here
stops here and only leave it when they marry or die.' She went to
England to work in the early 1960s, and on her return tried for a job
in Rathborne's. Betty finds the work hard but very rewarding. 'The
piecework was tough going but paid well. They still have the very
old ways of doing things. I remember hand-dipping the candles in
dye and getting paid an extra one penny per hour for it – and twelve
pennies or a shilling made up just five pence in today's money.' Betty
fondly recalls a visit to Germany to view machines that the company

Betty Byrne showing her work to a school party

(PHOTO BERNARD NEARY)

was purchasing: 'I went to Dusseldorf with Monica and other workers. We saw all the machinery including the wick-making machine. It was a great learning experience. Of course, the hard work is still there and anytime that there is a threatened ESB strike we're working here day and night.'

Following in the family tradition, Greta McGauley, who retired in April 1995, spent thirty years at Rathborne's – her mother Margaret Moore worked for the company as an office cleaner from 1951 to 1974, and her brother Noel Moore and sisters Kathleen Boyle and Rosaleen Vickers worked in the factory. Kathleen was a forewoman and though she left on marriage, came back and worked with the firm for a further five years. 'My cousin Eileen Moore also worked at the factory, in the 1930s, with Maureen Barrett and Nellie Brennan.' Greta packed and wrapped the candles: 'When I retired we were wrapping the candles in cellophane, but up to 1984 we were using brown paper.' She has only fond memories of Rathborne's: 'They were a good firm. I miss the place terrible.'

Richard (Dick) Corcoran from Emmet Road, Inchicore, spent nearly thirty-five years with the firm, joining just after Hugh Eimer McCormick took over at the helm and retiring in 1980 when he reached 65 years of age – 'I retired on Friday at four o'clock and I was 65 at ten o'clock that night.' A former hurler with Eoghan Ruadh (now St Oliver Plunkett–Eoghan Ruadh GAA Club) he was a steward at Croke Park, at the Hogan Stand, from 1929 until 1995. He keeps in close touch with affairs at Rathborne's and knows all the comings and goings, retirements and promotions at East Wall. He looks forward to his annual visit from production manager Joe Brennan, who brings the firm's Christmas gift of a bottle of whiskey and a supply of candles. He recalls his time at East Wall:

> I started in Rathborne's just after the war and I got the job because Mick Flanagan, who came from Blanchardstown and had worked in the old factory at Castleknock, had died and there was a vacancy in the gate office. The city deliveries were carried out by horse-and-cart and there were two big, heavy horses stabled where the present factory shop is located. One horse was white and he was called Snowball and the other, a red one, was called Barney. Around 1950 we changed over to motor trucks and the stables were converted into a unit for floral-candle production. I got the 24 bus into work from my house in Inchicore to the top of East Wall Road. In the early 1950s I bought a James 125cc motor bike for £40. I worked with some great fellows – Mick Stewart, who was a gentleman, Larry Byrne, Mick Flood, Terry Monaghan, who became a great friend of mine, Johnny Grant, John Bell, who worked in the melting house, George Tinkle and Paddy Ward, both fitters, Mickey Bell, who worked in the dispatch area and was just a boy when he started, Jimmy and Gerry English, who like Mick Stewart were Blanchardstown men. These were all Rathborne people, as were Ann Gaughan, Vincent Armstrong and Joey Entwhistle, who worked in the office. It was a very busy factory then and nearly 200 people worked there and during busy periods they even took on casual workers.
>
> I was promoted to the dispatch area in the mid-1950s and I spent the rest of my working life there. At any time

Larry Byrne filling a candle-moulding machine, 1949

we had 600 tons of candles in stock, and the stores were
very impressive, with wooden boxes containing 72 pounds
weight of candles and the top nailed down, stacked up to
eighteen high against the walls. In the early 1960s they
switched from wooden to cardboard cartons and the
number of candles was reduced to 32 pounds of candles in
each carton. The brands we produced at the time included
the Gem, which came in six colours and in six- and four-
inch sizes, and Venetian, again in six colours and in
twelve- and eight-inch sizes. The Gem was a beautiful,
square half-pound red candle and I have two of them on
my mantelpiece which are over thirty years old. Around
1963 we got a lucrative South African order and we were
working flat out to meet it. I remember it well, each week
I used to load up two containers of candles, carrying the
Peacock and Ship brand-name, for South Africa. Into the
container we loaded 1308 cartons, with fifty cartons on a
pallet.

Also now retired from the trade is Christy Moran from Maywood Avenue in Raheny. He started work in Rathborne's in 1949 after spending the war years in the army and some years as paymaster in Fuel Importers Limited. He worked in Rathborne's until his retirement in 1983 and recalls his career:

> It was a small company [when I started]. H.E. McCormick was the managing director and Niall Sheerin, who'd sell horse-dung to a stable, was the sales director. It was a great job, the wages were good, they arranged my mortgage and repayments were deducted from my salary. The work environment was terrific – it was like a home to me. I worked in the dispatch and purchasing and customs clearance areas. During the 1950s we had a thriving market in the US, in South Africa and many other countries. There were over seventy people working there when I started. We all worked as a team and when Lalor's joined us they fitted in really well. I worked with some great people – Joe Brennan and Tadgh O'Leary who came from Lalor's, Louis Ingoldsby, Vincent Armstrong, Victor Hughes, Bobby Leppla, Jack McCann and John Roche. Do you know that they send a parcel out to me every Christmas?

Joining Rathborne's at fourteen years of age, Patricia Mulhall has now spent over forty years at East Wall. Her two sisters, Angela and Joanna, also worked at the factory, and her own work included the preparation and packaging of night lights, putting seventy-two lights on each tray. Early in her career she went on to piece work, which was very hard but financially rewarding:

> My brother Christopher Mulhall worked here and when I started I was earning thirty-one shillings a week. My hours were 8 a.m. to 5 p.m. and when I turned eighteen years my hours were 8 a.m. to 6 p.m. I spent years working on birthday candles, tipping and packing them. We packed six different colours of candles into the presentation box, then wrapped the boxes by the dozen in

brown paper. We sealed the brown paper with glue, which we made ourselves. Mick Flood used to hand-make night lights and I remember being fascinated at him piercing them. We made our own cardboard boxes and also paper tubes for packing the candles. I remember Vera Donnelly and Jane Reilly, who were great at making up boxes.

At the tender age of nineteen, Tommy Rock commenced work 'on the candles' at Lalor's, in 1951. 'My first week's wage was three pounds and fifteen shillings.' His first duties included scraping wax off the floor, making tapers and nailing the packaging boxes. 'With Liz Nicholson I started to make quarter-inch candles on a drum and we used to tip them ourselves with a knife.' Tommy remembers when, as a young single man, his own family home was lit by candlelight: 'We lived in Love Lane in Ballybough. We had an oil light downstairs in the house and upstairs was lit by candle. We didn't get in the electricity until after the war.' Tommy bought an NSU Quigley motor bike from his brother for just £10 to commute to work. He first started making machine candles in 1955 in Lalor's

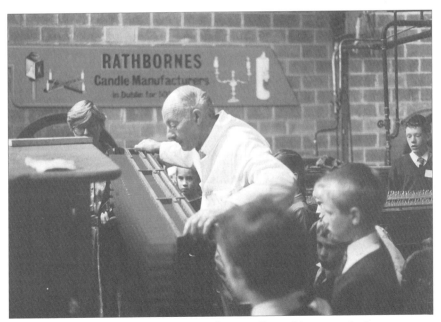

Tommy Rock demonstrating machine candle-making to a school tour
(PHOTO BERNARD NEARY)

Strand Street premises, and a Mr Fitzgerald later trained him how to make beeswax candles. When Lalor's amalgamated with Rathborne's in 1966 a lot of his workmates retired as they were then over sixty-five years old. He welcomed the move: 'Rathborne's were far better employers. I bought a car when we moved, a second-hand Austin for £40. The insurance was only £25 and I got the petrol in work; they gave me three gallons every week for £1.' Tommy would be familiar to hundreds of people, schoolchildren and adults alike, as he was the one who, during school, group and tourist visits to the factory, was assigned to the demonstration of the production of machine-candles, manufactured on the machines that were originally installed in the old Dunsinea plant during the 1800s.

During the bitter winter of 1947 John Mackey of East Wall – whose sister Annie Mackey also worked at the firm – started working in Rathborne's for nineteen shillings a week. When he retired in the summer of 1997 he was the longest-serving worker on the books:

> I started as a wooden box maker with Willie Ingles and we were put working with Tony and Harry McLoughlin and Billy Lindsay. We had a printing stamp and we put the purchasing-company's name on the wooden boxes. It was funny, because people would say to me that 'such-and-such's candles are better than yours' and they would all be Rathborne candles. Like today, the factory was always kept spotless and I remember Mick Mooney had the job of scraping the floor. The girls stopped at 5.15 p.m. and had then to scrub their benches. From all the scrubbing over the years the wood in the benches was the colour of milk.

John recalls the foreman Jack Reilly, who lived on the premises: 'He was a great, friendly character and he was the first one we would see every day, for in those days the foreman always resided within the factory gates.' John left the box-making to 'go on the candles in 1966, because when a job in the factory became vacant, it went on the board for three days and workers could put their name down for it. I put my name down and got the job.' He worked in the Melting House and 'this is where I was when the *Hands* TV documentary was being filmed in 1980'. The documentary starts off with John mixing and melting the wax and pumping it to the vats. The melted wax was piped from the vats around the factory and let out into the production areas by releasing valves. He picked out his wax mix with Tony Bell before throwing it into the vat to begin the melting process.

Love Is in the Air

There once was a slogan for a well-known Dublin nightclub in the 1970s which ran: 'Love stories begin at Zhivago's.' It could equally be said that 'Love stories begin at Rathborne's.' One of the staff reels off the list of romances which first took root in the factory: 'John Mackey married Theresa Tracey; John Bell married Annie O'Brien; Gerry O'Brien married Ann Stanley; Christy O'Brien married Sara Kinsella; Ritchie Grant married Martha McBride;

Rathborne's, East Wall, 1930s

Rita Foley married Tom Hughes; Jack McCann the foreman married Ann McAuley; and Terry Monaghan married Pattie O'Reilly.' Of course the company helped by giving free outings to places like Arklow and Courtown during the summers of the 1950s and 1960s, and it was on such outings that many romances blossomed.

The dispatch area is handled by Michael Bell form Artane, whose father and mother, John Bell and Ann O'Brien, also worked at the plant: 'My brother Tony used to work here and he is with me in the *Hands* documentary, you can see us both throwing the solid wax into the vat for melting.' Michael continues a long family tradition of working in the company, for his grandfather, also named Michael, worked for Rathborne's. Michael has given twenty-seven years' service to the firm and recalls his early years, when the plastic holders for the votive lights were returned to be cleaned and ready for re-use. His duties have included recycling the plastic holders and scraping the floors of wax. He is now assigned to dispatch duties: 'I look after deliveries of candles by rail, courier and company van and also look after exports; our main business is still church-based, but that is quickly being matched by sales to restaurants and souvenir sales.'

Tadhg O'Leary was with the company for almost forty-six years. He started his working life with Lalor's, based in Cork and looking after sales in the southern region. A native of that city, he came to Dublin with a young family following the amalgamation with Rathborne's and was responsible for the company's sales to nearly two hundred parishes around Ireland. Retired since the autumn of 1996, he enjoyed 'a happy and productive working life' in the industry and still maintains links with the company. Michael Duffy has taken over Tadhg's responsibilities. Another former employee is Helen Coyle from East Wall, who spent eight years with the firm, leaving around 1979: 'I worked with Gretta Moore, Rita Carroll, Monica Stewart, Betty Byrne, Joe Brennan and Bobby Leppla, both Lalor men, and Terry Monaghan, who was an awful messer – you'd always get a great laugh when he was around. Jack McCann was good to work with. My supervisor was Maureen Barrett, who was an extremely fair lady. The manager, Niall Sheerin, was gas. I worked packing night-lights and candles before being appointed to the staff canteen. A great crowd from East Wall worked in the factory when I was there and I really enjoyed going into work. The craic was always great and I was very happy there.' Pat McElwaine also enjoys the craic at the factory and really enjoys her working life at Rathborne's. She has been with the company for nearly twenty years now and is currently a machine operator on the votive candle line. She lives on Forth Road in East Wall and is originally from Foley Street. She started with the firm in 1979 'making the block candles – the St Martin candles – cutting, fluffing and packing them'.

'Where is the time gone? I have been here for forty-three years and it flew,' exclaims Joe Brennan, originally from Benburb Street and now living in Drimnagh. Joe started in Lalor's in 1952, working in the dispatch and general works area. In 1985 he became production manager, a position he still holds. During his time modern plant machinery was installed and the whole factory modernised. 'As a result of the modernisation, productivity increased by 66 per cent and allowed great flexibility. The machinery is so sophisticated that we can quickly change from one product process to another.' While enthusing over the modern processes, Joe thinks it is great to see the handmade tradition continuing – 'and that is what the public want. Hand-made candles are increasing in popularity every year and any visitor to the factory wants to see how they are made. I find it fascinating to watch Bobby Leppla hand-making candles in the age-old tradition from the vantage point of a state-of-the-art, ultramodern candle-making machine which churns out

Joe Brennan checking the finished product
(PHOTO DAVID SHAW-SMITH

candles by the hundreds.' One of the many highlights in Joe's career at the company was the making of the Dublin Millennium Candle in 1988:

> We had to deliver it by special trailer, taking it from the factory at six in the morning. Carmencita Hederman, the Lord Mayor, was very good to the workers who tended to the candle, which burned outside the Mansion House for the year. One night the candle was blown out during a storm and Gaybo was pestered by phone calls to his radio show. Over the airwaves he asked us, 'Will you ever go over there and light it?' We also make the big Amnesty International candle and that is really a treat to work on.

A unique feature of Rathborne's is the identifying of people who work there as a 'Lalor' or a 'Rathborne' person. This trait runs through all layers of the firm; Tommy Rock immediately described himself as a 'Lalor man' and Eimer McCormick, former managing director, when inquiring about the author's interviews at the factory, described each person mentioned in conversation as a 'Lalor' or a 'Rathborne' person.

It is fitting to bring this history of Rathborne's to a close with a man who is a rarity in modern society, for he is doing the exact same job, in exactly the same fashion, that his predecessors have been doing since the foundation of the company over 500 years ago. Bobby Leppla is a master candle-maker who has featured in many a newspaper, magazine and journal over his working life. Originally from Patrick Street on Dublin's south side (not far from where Rathborne's first set up business in Dublin over 500 years ago), he attended St Francis CBS as a boy, leaving school at twelve years of age to work with a local shoemaker for ten shillings a week. The following year he left to take up work in Lalor's for one pound a week:

> I started off working on the candles by looking after five craft candle-makers, some in their seventies, one in his early eighties – remember that in those days there was no compulsory retirement. I spent seven years working to

these men before I became qualified to hand-make candles and was twenty-one years of age by the time I got to make my first candle. I am now the only full-time hand-craft candle-maker with the company, as handmade candles form only part of the duties of the other candle-makers. I have been with the firm for over fifty years now and I work mainly with beeswax. In early springtime I am always working flat out on Paschal candles for church and religious clients. Candlemas and Advent are other busy times when life for me here at the plant gets really hectic.

He made the candle for the Marian Year in 1954, which stood lighting in O'Connell Street in a special casing. That casing is now incorporated in the Marian shrine in Dominick Street, in Dublin's city centre. 'It was quite a difficult job. The candle was sixteen foot in length and twelve inches in diameter. We had to get up on ladders to make it.' He recalls some of the trade's great candle-makers, including Terry Monaghan, Eddie Stringer, Paddy Murtagh and Dominick Redmond.

Watching Bobby work is like stepping back in time. The carousel with which he makes the handmade candles was purchased by the company in 1932 – the year of the Eucharistic Congress, when the firm could not keep up with the demand. Conscious of his strong links with the trade, he 'absolutely loves the work, it is all handwork and great teamwork'. His hidden hand has been a part of certain aspects of Irish historic occasions – for instance he 'hand-made the

Paddy Murtagh checks a clamp of red candles. Paddy has been working with candles since he was sixteen

(PHOTO DAVID SHAW-SMITH)

candles, in unbleached beeswax and each one thirty-six inches long, for the lying-in-state of the body of President Eamon de Valera'.

When he first came in contact with Rathborne's, the author could not believe how happy all the staff were with their work and at their work – they all seemed part of one big family. It is rare nowadays, particularly in the manufacturing and administrative sector, to find such fulfilment. Speaking to the staff and watching them work, the author was inclined to believe that it is the connection with the past, with the provision of simple candlelight, which has been with us now for thousands of years, that brings such satisfaction to those working in Rathborne's. Looking at Bobby examining the hand-

crafted beeswax candles, and at Monica carefully hand-wrapping each individual wax candle for the special Superquinn order, the idea of the connection with an age-old tradition is reinforced. It is not inconceivable that in 500 years' time, when the task of recording a thousand years of the company is being undertaken, people at the future plant will be carrying out their work in exactly the same fashion – and with the same pleasure – as Bobby and Monica and everyone else at Rathborne's does today.

Bobby Leppla, master chandler, at work on wax candles

Will of Joseph Rathborne, 1737

In the name of God Amen I Joseph Rathborne of the city of Dublin Chandler being of sound mind and memory (praise be to God) do make my last will as followeth. I recommend my soul to God hoping for mercy through the mediation of my Saviour Jesus Christ and my body to the earth to be interred in the parish churchyard of Clontarf or in the parish churchyard of St. Mary's which my children as my executors shall think fit. I desire that my just debts and funeral expenses be first paid.

I leave unto my son Richard Rathborne the house and backside on the strand at Abbey Street wherein Mrs. St. Florence now dwells with two lots of ground thereto adjoining, each containing about fifty two feet front, one of which lots is now waste and the other set to Moses and Hugh Darly, and I do hereby charge the said house and two lots of ground with the payment of the yearly rent of fourteen pounds (being part of the yearly rent of twenty pounds thereout in alia) payable to Col. Shepheard. I also leave my said son Richard Rathborne ten pounds sterling for mourning. I leave unto my son William Rathborne the full benefit of the lease for years which I hold under Mr. John Moland of concerns in St. Mary's Lane subject to the yearly rent thereout payable. I also leave unto my said son William ten pounds for mourning. Item.

I leave unto Mr. Jeremiah Standring and Mr. Joseph West the corner house adjoining the said Mrs. St. Florence's said holding wherein Edward Mathews lately dwelt, and also the small house in Liffey Street adjoining the backside of the said last mentioned house, and built by the said Edward Mathews (being the remainder of the premises held under the lease from the said Col. Shepheard) subject to the payment of six pounds per annum to the said Col. Shepheard being the remainder of the said yearly rent of twenty pounds in trust and to the intent to pay and apply the clear yearly rents issues and profits of both the said houses to such use and uses as my daughter Mary Crampton, wife of Philip Crampton,

Bookseller, shall direct, separate and apart from her said husband and over which he shall have no power nor shall the same be liable to his debts or control during the natural life of my said daughter Mary and from and after her decease. To the intent that the benefit from the same two houses shall go to my daughter Catherine Rathborne, her executors, administrators and assignees during the remainder of the term of years which shall be then to come therein. I also leave unto my said daughter Mary and to my said son-in-law Philip Crampton ten pounds for mourning for them both. Item. I leave unto my said daughter Catherine the house, backhouse and backside in Drumcondra Lane now in the tenancy of Major Carmichael subject to the payment of thirty shillings per annum thereout to Mr. Christopher Dominick from whom I hold the same (in alia). Item.

I leave unto my daughter Dorothy Rathborne the house and garden adjoining the said last mentioned house and now in the tenancy of Andrew Aickman, she paying thereout thirty shillings per annum to the said Dominick and permitting the shore of the said adjoining house to run under the entry of the said Aickman's said house as it now doth and giving liberty to open and cleanse the said shore and paying one moiety on half of the charge of opening and cleansing the same when necessary. I also leave unto my said daughter Dorothy the house and garden in Drumcondra Lane now in the tenancy of Mrs. Wallace, she paying thereon forty shillings per annum being one half of the ground rent payable thereout. I also leave unto my daughter Catherine the house and backside wherein Mrs. Wybrant's now dwells adjoining the last mentioned house, she paying thereout forty shillings per annum being the other half of the ground rent thereof. I also leave unto my said two daughters Catherine and Dorothy forty pounds apiece. Item. I leave unto my daughter Alice Rathborne the full benefits of two leases for years—viz—one of which I hold under Charles Campbell of concerns in Drumcondra Lane and the other lease which I hold under Sir John Eccles of ground in Drogheda Street subject to the yearly rents by the said leases respectively reserved. I also leave unto my said daughter Alice the sum of forty pounds. Item.

I leave unto my son Joseph Rathborne the interest and benefit of three leases—viz. one lease which I hold for years from Valentine Prendergast and Mary Vincent of a house and concerns at the corner of Mary's Abbey, Dublin, one other lease being for lives renewable forever of the house and concerns in Mary's Abbey wherein I now live and which I hold under Mr. John Kerr and Mr. Robert Sisson of the concerns whereon my workhouse is now erected subject to the yearly rents by the said leases reserved. I also leave unto my said son Joseph all my working tools, three pans, set, trough and other implements belonging to my said workhouse (but no part of the stock therein) and it is my will that an inventory of the said working tools and implements be taken immediately after my death to the intent that the same may be preserved for my said son Joseph when of age. But it is my will that the said demise to my said son Joseph is upon this careful condition that he do and shall exercise and follow the Trade of a Tallow-Chandler for ten years from my decease otherwise the benefit of the said three leases and all my working tools, Pans, Trough and other implements aforementioned be sold and the money arising by such sale shall go and be divided amongst my said sons Richard and William and my said daughters Catherine, Dorothy and Alice equally. Item. I also leave unto my said son Joseph the sum of one hundred and fifty pounds together with Mr. Robt. Gibsons bond for £50 and all interest due thereon and which bond judgement hath been entered in the court of Exchequer. Item. It is my will that if the said son Joseph shall die before the age of 21 years without issue then what is hereby left him shall go to his two brothers, Richard and William equally between them. Item. I leave six pounds to the children of Thomas Barton late of the town of Drogheda, merchant. I leave five pounds to my three executors for a piece of mourning. Item. I leave unto my dear wife Katherine one hundred and fifty pounds and all my plate and household goods. Item.

As to the lease of the house and lands of Clontarf which I hold under John Vernon Exq. and as to the lease and concerns in Great Britain Street which I hold under Mr. John Brock subject to the ground rents of the same it is my will that my said dear wife shall hold and enjoy the same and receive the profits thereof during her life if she so long continues a widow in which she may dispose thereof at her death among such of my said children as she shall think fit, but if she marries again I leave both the said lease and the premises thereby demised and the benefit thereof to my said three daughters – Katherine, Dorothy and Alice to be equally divided amongst them. As to the rest Residue and remainder of my worldly goods effects and substance whatsoever Real or personal not herein disposed of I leave to my said dear wife Katherine her Heirs etc. And it is my will that in case my effects will not be sufficient to answer my debts and legacys then I order that my wife and children shall bear a part of such deficiency in proportion to the legacy hereby left them respectively, the legacy to my said daughter Mary Crampton and her husband excepted. Item. It is my will that if such person or persons as are indebted to me in small sums of money shall in the opinion of my executors appear to be poor and indigent then it is my will to remit such debts. Item.

If any difference shall arise between my respective children I order that the same shall be determined by any two of my executors whose determination therein shall be final. And if any of my said children shall refuse to submit to such determination then I order that such child or children so refusing shall forfeit the legacy left therein. And then the same shall go to and be equally divided amongst the remainder of my said children. And I certify that I do hereby constitute and appoint my said wife Katherine during her widowhood but no longer, the said Jeremiah Standering and Joseph West executors of this my last will, hereby revoking all former wills by me. Spoken in witness whereof two parts of this my will both of the same tenor and date I have subscribed my name and affixed my seal, the tenth day of November in the year of Our Lord, one thousand seven hundred and thirty-seven.

(Signed) Joseph Rathborne. *(Signed)* Witnesses.

APPENDIX II

Tallow-Chandlers Guild

A guild was a medieval mutual-benefit association and the term is derived from the old German word *geld* or *gelt* meaning a payment. Successive generations of the Rathborne family were members of The Guild of Tallow Chandlers, Soap Boilers and Wax-Light Makers. This organisation, twelfth in order of precedence in the Dublin City Assembly, was founded in 1538 by civic charter and was granted a royal charter in 1674 (26 Charles II). The order of precedence was determined by the antiquity of the guild. Each guild had its own patron saint, and the swearing-in day – the day assigned for new guild members to take the oaths of supremacy and uniformity – usually coincided with the feast of that patron saint. In the case of the candle-makers, swearing-in was conducted on the feast of St George (23rd April).

Like all guilds, the tallow-chandlers guild had its own distinctive colours, blue and sky-blue, which were displayed on banners carried in public procession, and were often worn by members as a cockade in their hats. A list of colours of each Dublin guild is given in a document dated 1767. Over the years the guild met in various city locations, including Carpenters' Hall, Corn Market (early 1700s) and Grafton Street (1783); from 1806 to 1841 it met in St Audeon's Arch, High Street.

St Audeon's Arch on the City Walls was built in 1240 and is the only surviving example of a gate in the medieval city walls. The guild of tanners was the first to hold meetings there, taking a lease of the Arch in 1616, which was renewed for ninety-nine years in 1675. Many other guilds met in the Arch, including the Tallow-Chandlers, holding their meetings in a tower above the arch, which was removed when the structure was restored in 1880 under the supervision of the architect Sir Thomas Drew. During European Architectural Heritage Year in 1975 St Audeon's Arch was again restored to its original form by Dublin Corporation.

Records surviving relating to the guild include the guild patent, dated 1678, a rare and fabulous document with a colour bust of Charles II, beautifully inscribed in pen and ink (National Library of Ireland Ms 9007) and minute books 1814 to 1840 (NLI Ms 80). Surviving transcripts include a copy of the nineteenth-century guild charter (NLI Ms 80) and *Notes on Tallow-Chandlers' Guild* (National Archives, TA 1439).

The power of the guilds reached its height in the mid-1700s but during the 1800s they began to lose influence in the areas of industry and commerce. With the loss of their political power following the passing of the Municipal Corporation Reform Act of 1840 obsolescence set in and the guilds, including the Tallow-Chandlers Guild, were wound up around 1841. Dublin Public Libraries have published a very interesting book entitled *Directory of Historic Dublin Guilds*, edited by Mary Clarke and Raymond Refauss (ISBN 0-94684-112x).

St Audeon's Arch, 1998

(PHOTO BERNARD NEARY)

APPENDIX III

Roll of Freemen of the City of Dublin 1468–1774
Rathborne Family Name

The ancient Freedom of Dublin was instituted at the time of the Norman conquest in the late twelfth century. Holders of the Freedom were known as Free Citizens and were entitled to significant trading privileges and the right to vote in municipal and parliamentary elections. Admission was granted by the Dublin City Assembly at the great feasts of Christmas, Easter, Midsummer and Michaelmas. To qualify it was usually necessary to have been born within the city boundaries and to be a member of one of the Dublin trade guilds. Under the Penal Laws Catholics were excluded from the Freedom of Dublin during the period 1691 to 1793.

Admission to the Freedom was granted in several ways: by service, to those who had completed an apprenticeship in one of the guilds; by birth, to sons and sometimes daughters of Free Citizens; by marriage, to sons-in-law of Free Citizens; by fine, to those willing to pay the hefty fee into the city treasury; by grace especial, an honorary Freedom; and by Act of Parliament, to 'encourage Protestant strangers to settle in Ireland'. This last category was granted to French Huguenots and English Quakers. Under the Representation of the People Act 1918 the ancient Freedom of Dublin was abolished to make way for a more democratic franchise. The name Rathborne appears on ten occasions in the lists of those admitted to the Freedom of Dublin during the period 1468 to 1774:

- 1651   Thomas Rathborne (Glover)
- 1654   John Rathborne (Glover)
- 1675   Willus Rathborne (Tailor)
- 1680   Hugo Rathborne (Butcher)
- 1681   Johes Rathborne junior (Glover)
- 1701   Joseph Rathburne (Chandler)

1714   William Rathborne, apprentice of Joseph Rathborne
        (Tallow Chandler)

1732   William Rathborne, son of Joseph Rathborne
        (Chandler)

1753   Joseph Rathborne, son of Joseph Rathborne
        (Chandler)

1762   Joseph Rathburne, by service with Philip Crampton
        (Merchant)

Candles were sold in many different sizes, and it was often impossible to fit one into a socket without wedging it with paper. Many patents were taken out for adjustable sockets, but according to his advertisement from the 'Ironmonger', 1861, Henry Loveridge had found an easier answer. A least one candle manufacturer, 'Pybus' of Derby and Bristol, added fins to candles to ensure a tight fit

Appendix IV

"Different Layers of Darkness"

A poor old gentleman went into the Vernon Gallery during the tremendous fog last week. He came out, however, directly afterwards, declaring that 'It was very strange, but I could see a great deal clearer outside in the fog.'

We can imagine it would be all the difference between Simple Fog and Compound Fog. We expect, some very black morning, to hear of the Vernon Gallery being completely stript, by two or three clever fellows having taken advantage of the fog to run off with all the pictures. The Trustees of the National Gallery will then have a light suddenly breaking in upon them, and will be able to see the darkness of their ways.

We should not at all wonder that they will then, when there is nothing more to see, order half a pound of candles. Up to that period, of course, 'le jeu ne vaut pas la chandelle'.

— *Punch*, London, February 1849

153

Rathborne's factory staff photo, 1952

Front row, l. to r.: Patty Fitzpatrick, Rosie Moore, Carmel O'Reilly, – Doyle, Frances Jordan, Martha McGuinness, Theresa McEvoy, Vera Manning, – Kavanagh, Vera Harris, Helen Whelan, Noreen Murray, Patty Mulhall, Maura Woods, Ann McAuley, Ellen Hughes, Angela Mulhall, Nuala Thornton, Florrie Kinsella

Middle row, l. to r.: Rose McBirney, Joe Magee, Joan Delaney, Joan Grant, Mary McLean, —, Vera Donnelly, Willie Ryan, Johnny Grant, Joan Cummins, Carmel Doring, Patty Fitzpatrick, Bridie Smith, Brenda Methcaff, Annie Mackey, Francis Kelly, John Bell, Freddie O'Toole, George Tinkle

Back row, l. to r.: Dick Corcoran, – O'Toole, Terry Monaghan, Patty O'Reilly, Mick Stewart, Billy Lindsay, Sam Smith, Pat Campbell, Rita Carroll, Johnny Mackey, Rosie Carroll, Betty Boshell, Margaret Ryan, Maureen Connolly, Noel Delaney, Mary Connolly, Rita Foley, Billy May, —, Bob McCormac, Christopher Mulhall, Jack Daly, Paddy Murtagh, – O'Toole, Larry Byrne

Appendix V

Irish Lighthouse Suppliers 1820–1829

During the period 1820 to 1829 best-quality spermaceti oil was the illuminant used at all Irish lighthouses. Henry Rathborne began supplying oil to the lighthouse service in 1820 and during the ensuing decade was the primary supplier and in some years the sole supplier. The oil was delivered to the lighthouse oil store at Lower Abbey Street, Dublin, from where it was distributed by the service to the various lighthouses around the coast of Ireland. The following is a schedule of some of the payment dates and amounts paid to Henry Rathborne during the period 1820 to 1829. During that period a total of fifty-four payments are listed in the Ballast Board's accounts totalling what was a huge sum for those times, £34,882=15=2d.

Date	Substance	Cost £ s d
01 June 1820	Spermaceti Oil	938- 1- 3
14 September 1820	Spermaceti Oil (5,028 gals)	1,642- 4- 2
07 April 1821	Spermaceti Oil	1,135- 4- 7
29 November 1821	Spermaceti Oil	215-19- 5
23 May 1822	Spermaceti Oil	935-19- 5
25 October 1822	Spermaceti Oil	167- 3- 2
27 March 1823	Spermaceti Oil	803- 0- 4
29 May 1823	Spermaceti Oil	1,886- 5- 5
17 June 1824	Spermaceti Oil	510- 7- 7
09 December 1824	Spermaceti Oil	93- 7-11
08 July 1825	Spermaceti Oil	800- 0- 0
27 October 1825	Spermaceti Oil	1,428-11- 8
18 May 1826	Spermaceti Oil	1,207-13- 6
25 May 1826	Spermaceti Oil	637-18- 3
26 April 1827	Spermaceti Oil	1,625- 1- 8

Date	Substance	Cost £ s d
10 May 1827	Spermaceti Oil	994- 8- 4
25 April 1828	Spermaceti Oil	1,169- 5- 0
07 August 1828	Spermaceti Oil	1,366- 1- 0
06 November 1828	Spermaceti Oil	325-10- 0
30 April 1829	Spermaceti Oil	1,027- 8- 9
5 June 1829	Spermaceti Oil	1,483- 8- 0
30 July 1829	Spermaceti Oil	506-13- 6

Note: Old currency of pounds, shillings and pence in use prior to decimalisation in the early 1970s; £1-0-0 equals £1.00; 10s or 10/= equals 50p; 5s or 5/= equals 25p; 1s (12 pennies or 12d) equals 5p; 4d equals 2p and 2d equals approximately 1p.

APPENDIX VI

Wages Schedule for Week Ending 6 January 1926

Location	Name	Time	Earnings £-s-d	Earnings less Health & Unemployment Deductions £ - s - d
Melting House	Connor M	48	2–14– 0 (o/t 4–3)	2–17– 2
	Morley W	48	1– 2– 0	1– 2– 0
	McKenna C	48	1–15– 0	1–13–11
Candle Making	Coates W		3–10– 0	3– 8–11
	Stewart M	48	3– 0– 0	2–18–11
	Daly M	48	2–14– 0	2–12–11
	Eustace K	48	10– 0	10– 0
	Molloy M	47	9–11	9–11
	Ridge Eileen	48	10– 0	10– 0
	Flanagan M	48	2–14– 0	2–12–11
	Reid M	48	4–18– 8 (o/t 5–0)	4– 2– 7
	Flood M	30	2– 6– 2	2– 5– 1
	Gregory J	48	2–14– 0	2– 5– 1
	Smith W	48	2–14– 0	2–12–11
	Horan T	48	3–11– 4	3–10– 3
	Kavanagh E	48	1–12– 1	1–11– 0
	Daly L	48	3– 8– 1 (o/t 1–4–1)	4–11– 1
	Hughes J	17	4– 4	4– 4
	Coyle J	48	2–14– 0	2–12–11
	English J	39	2– 4– 0	2– 2–11
	Mooney D	48	19– 0	18– 4
	Cunningham P	48	2–14– 0	2–12–11
	Byrne L	47	11–11	11–11
	Daly J	48	2–14– 0	2–12–11
	Reilly W	43	1– 2– 0 (o/t 9–9)	1–16– 4
	Purcell C	48	1– 2– 0	1– 1– 1
Candle Packing	Doherty Sarah	48	1– 3– 6	1– 2–11
	Stradman Kathleen	48	13–10	13–10
	Kinsella Eileen	48	1– 5– 5	1– 4– 7
	Frye Hilda	43	9– 9	9– 9
	O Donnell Lily	48	1– 0– 4	9– 9
	Rockcliffe, Isobella	48	12– 3	12– 3
	Redmond Kathleen	48	1– 0– 0	19– 9
	Lawless Rita	48	10– 0	10– 0
	Mahon Nellie	48	1– 0– 0	19– 3

Location	Name	Time	Earnings	Earnings less Health & Unemployment Deductions
			£-s-d	£ - s - d
Candle Packing contd.	Brown Ellen	48	1– 5– 0	1– 4– 2
	Mason Catherine	47	9–11	9–11
	Whelan Dora	48	10– 0	10– 0
	McGehan Maureen	48	10– 0	10– 0
	Conroy Nora	48	10– 0	10– 0
	English C	48	2–14– 0	2–12–11
	Bollard G	48	1– 8– 0	1– 8– 0
	Lindsay W	48	2–14– 0	2–12–11
	Daly J	39	2– 8– 4	2– 7– 3
	Lindsay J	48	2–14– 0	2–12–11
Case Making	O Brien M	48	1– 2– 0	1– 1– 0
	Caffrey J	48	19– 0	18– 4
	McCann F	48	10– 0	10– 0
	McEntee P	48	17– 0	16– 4
Stoking	Byrne J	48	3– 0– 0 (o/t 1–11–11)	4–10–10
Repairs	Holland F	48	3– 0– 0 (o/t 1– 6– 7)	4– 5– 6
	O Brien M	48	2–14– 0 (o/t 1–3–11)	3–16–10
	Carroll T	44	3– 0– 0 (o/t 1–7– 4)	4– 2– 7
Warehousing	Duncan W	48	2–14– 0	2–12–11
	McEntee L	47	1– 9– 4	1– 8– 6
	Broderick	48	2–15– 0	2–14– 3
Carters	Perricoth G	48	2–19– 0 (o/t 5–3)	3– 3– 2
	Brennan J	48	2–19– 0 (o/t 8–0)	3– 5–11
	English J	51	3– 0– 0 (o/t 1– 4– 1)	3– 3– 0
Miscellaneous	Reilly C	48	2–19– 0	2–17–11
	Kealy J	48	2–14– 0	2–12–11
	Kelly P	48	3– 0– 6	2–19– 5
	Stoole E	48	2–14– 0	2–12–11
Pensioner	Connor M		1–10– 0	1–10– 0
Total			130–4–10	127–16–0

Written sources

Ball, Francis Erlington – *A History of County Dublin* and *Communication between London and Dublin from the 13th Century*

Belfast Municipal Art Gallery and Museum *Quarterly Notes*

Campbell, R. – *The London Tradesman* (1747)

Camphill Community – *A Candle on the Hill*, edited by Cornelius Pietzner

Card, Peter W. – *Early Vehicle Lighting*

Chambers Encyclopedia

Cork Examiner

Cheshire Records Office – Shire records

Chester City Records Office

Chronicle – Chester newspaper

City Archives Office, Dublin Corporation, City Hall, Dublin 2

Civic Museum, South William Street, Dublin 2

Clewyd Records Office

Commissioners of Irish Lights

Companies Office, Dublin

Cosgrave, Dillon – *North Dublin City & Environs* (1909)

Darley, James J. – *Know and Enjoy Tropical Fruit*

Dictionary of National Biography

Dublin Builder

Dublin Evening Mail

Eveleigh, David J. – *Candle Lighting*

Farrell, Valentine – *Not So Much to One Side*

Higgs, P.G., and J. Kewley – *Modern Uses of Paraffin Wax*

Irish Builder

Irish Independent

Irish Industrial Journal

Irish Labour History Society – *Saothar*

Irish Press

Irish Times

Irish Wholesale Grocer

National Library of Ireland

National Museum

Ó Crothán, Tomás – *An t-Oileánach*

Pearson, Lynn F. – *Lighthouses*

Representative Church Body, Churchtown (Library)

RGDATA – *Review*

Royal Cornish Gazette

Scoil Oilibhéir, Coolmine, Dublin 15 – Entries for 1996 School Project Competition on Candles, by Orla Ní Loinsigh and Brian O'Sullivan

Teahan, John – *Irish Silver: A Guide to the Exhibition*

Thom's Directory

Valuation Office Records

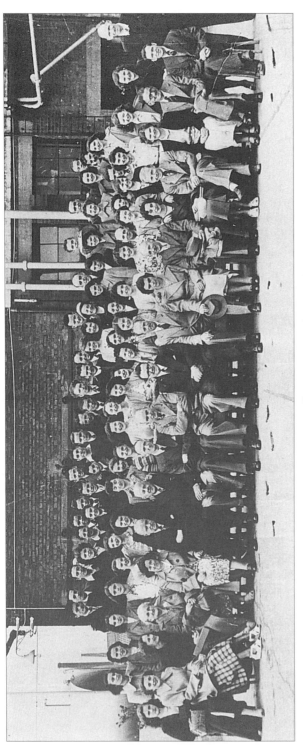

Rathborne's staff outing to Arklow, 1950.

Back row: —, —, – O'Reilly, J. Daly, M. Longbrey, J. Roche, J. English, M. McLoughlin, P. Flanaghan, – Ingle, S. Smyth, A. Meade, J. Mackey, – English, M. Flanaghan, —, J. Bell, M. Reade, —, A. O'Brien, N. Sheerin, – Byrne, —, L.Byrne, P. Murtagh, F. O'Toole, – O'Toole, K. Reddin, – Lindsay

Middle Row: —, L. Brunton, M. Bruton, V. Donnelly, A. Mulhall, C. Gray, —, M. Barrett, R. Carroll, C. Hannigan, P. Horan, E. Hughes, —, M. Connolly, F. Kinsella, B. Meade, B. Smyth, J. Magee, B. Boshell, J. Reilly, T. Treacy, M. Heffernan, W. Reilly

Front Row: B. Woods, A. Molsek, P. Reilly, – Monaghan, M. Stewart, E. Lacy, M. Stewart, J. Reilly, W. Carey, H.E. McCormick, J. Entwhistle, M. Whyte, G. Gleeson, G. Hughes, C. Moran, – Fuller, E. Fuller, G. Tinkler